# *Empower Your Kids To Be Adults*

## A Guide For Parents, Ministers, and Other Mentors

# Empower Your Kids To Be Adults

## A Guide For Parents, Ministers, and Other Mentors

Donald M. Joy, Ph.D.

**Evangel
Publishing House**
Nappanee, Indiana

*Empower Your Kids To Be Adults:*
*A Guide For Parents, Ministers, and Other Mentors*

Toll-free Order Line: (800) 253-9315
Internet Website: www.evangelpublishing.com

Scripture quotations, unless otherwise noted, are from HOLY BIBLE, NEW INTER-NATIONAL VERSION®. Copyright © 1973, 1978, 1984 by International Bible Society. Used by permission of Zondervan Publishing House. All rights reserved.

Scripture quotations identified as NKJV are from *The New King James Version*. Copyright © 1979, 1980, 1982, Thomas Nelson, Inc., Publishers.

Cover Design: Ted Ferguson

**Publisher's Cataloging-in-Publication**
*(Provided by Quality Books, Inc.)*
Joy, Donald M. (Donald Marvin), 1928-
    Empower your kids to be adults : a guide for parents, ministers, and other mentors / Donald M. Joy. – 1st ed.
    p. cm.
    Includes index.
    LCCN: 99-69351
    ISBN: 0-928915-01-9

    1. Mentoring.  2. Parenting–Religious aspects–Christianity. 3. Adolescent psychology  4. Interpersonal relations—Religious aspects—Christianity.    I. Title.
BV4597.52.J69 2000                  253.5
                                     QBI99-500575

Printed in the United States of America
1  2  3  4  5  EP  5  4  3  2  1

Saluting
the heroes of my own journey
from child to adult:

Marvin and Marie Royer Joy, my parents

Eugene Layman, my minister confidant

Mary Ruth Crown, my music mentor

Adrian Fields, my manly mentor

Books by Don Joy available from Evangel Publishing House:

*Bonding: Relationships in the Image of God*

*Empower Your Kids to Be Adults: A Guide for Parents,*
*Ministers, and Other Mentors*

*Men Under Construction*

*Re-bonding: Preventing and Restoring Damaged Relationships*


Books available from the author:

*Becoming a Man*

*Celebrating the New Woman*

*Lovers: Whatever Happened to Eden?*

*Meaningful Learning in the Church*

*Moral Development Foundations*

*Parents, Kids, and Sexual Integrity*

*Risk-Proofing Your Family*

*The Holy Spirit and You*

*Unfinished Business: How a Man Can Make Peace With His Past*

*Walk On!*

*Women at Risk*

Center for the Study of the Family
600 North Lexington Avenue
Wilmore, KY 40390
(606) 858-3817
don_joy@asburyseminary.edu

# Contents

# List of Figures

# Foreword

In a recent article in *U. S. News and World Report,* Joannie Schrof observed a subtle shift that has occurred in American society. While we have always recognized that adults have a special responsibility to protect and guide children, more recently local cities and states have begun to pass laws that *require* parents and guardians to take responsibility for their children. While such a shift from a moral imperative to a legal requirement may be subtle to some, Christians are increasingly aware that the institutional reinforcements that have historically been a part of culture are faltering at every turn. Schools, scouts, sports, and even youth groups provide no sure guarantee of mentoring and support for young people in their pilgrimage from childhood to adulthood. Increasingly parents, ministers, and other mentors have to intentionally create and promote the means by which young people are empowered to become adults.

That is why *Empower Your Kids To Be Adults* and the ideas and resources it provides are so important. We parents need all the help we can get!

I have known Don Joy now for nearly twenty-five years. I first met Don in my own young adult years. Later he became a mentor, colleague, confidant, and friend. As our relationship has broadened and deepened, I have continually been amazed and appreciative of his (and Robbie's) deep commitment to mentoring.

What is present in these pages is not a theoretical treatise on an interesting subject or an attempt to capitalize on a cultural trend with a quick fix book. This is wisdom born of experience shared in practical, honest, and personal ways. I know many of the people mentioned in this book. There are few superstars, no prima donnas. These are people in the trenches seeking to be good stewards of the lives with which they have been entrusted. These are people making a difference in ways that will bear *eternal* fruit.

After more than twenty years of youth ministry and ministry on the university campus, I thought I might be prepared to parent a teenager. I was wrong. I need all the help I can get. Fortunately, in this book, help is at hand.

One should not read this book for a prescriptive, "cookbook" answer to America's teen crisis. It should be read knowing that it will spawn ideas, create brainstorms, cause personal reflection, and encourage us for the task at hand. Perhaps of equal importance, it will remind us that indeed it does take a village to raise a child. Long before Hillary Clinton made the phrase popular, the people of Israel reminded one another that transformation occurred when truth and values were a part of the fabric of the child's family experience:

> Fix these words of mine in your hearts and minds; tie them as symbols on your hands and bind them on your foreheads. Teach them to your children, talking about them when you sit at home and when you walk along the road, when you lie down and when you get up. Write them on the doorframes of your houses and on your gates, so that your days and the days of your children may be many in the land that the Lord swore to give your forefathers, as many as the days that the heavens are above the earth. (Deut. 11:18-21).

While the homogeneity of the Jewish tribe and the boundaries of an agrarian culture are not present today, the importance of the matrix of relationships supporting young people still applies. Ira Schwartz, dean of the University of Pennsylvania, suggests that in fact parents have a benefit not available in families or cultures of the past: the benefit of choice. Parents and significant mentors can choose to involve themselves and others in children's lives in incredible ways if only they will! As Dr. Joy points out, in spite of the barrage of media programming that casts verbal and behavioral disrespect on adults, young people *overwhelmingly* say two of their greatest desires are to have a mentor and to please their parents!

One of my favorite writers is a Jewish poet and storyteller, Noah Ben Shea. In one of his books, *Jacob the Baker*, he tells the parable of "Jacob and the Children."

> After dinner, the children turned to Jacob and asked if he would tell them a story. "A story about what?" asked Jacob.
>
> "About a giant," squealed the children.
>
> Jacob smiled, leaned against the warm stones at the side of the fireplace, and began, his voice turning softly inward.
>
> "Once there was a boy who asked his father to take him to see the great parade that passed through the village where they lived. The father, remembering the parade from when he was a boy, quickly agreed, and the next morning the boy and his father set out together.

"As they approached the route the parade would take, people started to push in from all sides, and the crowd grew thick. When the people along the way became almost a wall, the father lifted his son and placed him on his shoulders.

"Soon the parade began, and as it passed, the boy kept telling his father how wonderful it was, how spectacular were the colors and images. The boy, in fact, grew so prideful of what he saw that he mocked those who saw less, saying even to his father, 'If only you could see what I see.'

"But," said Jacob, staring straight into the faces of the children, "what the boy did not look at was why he could see. What the boy forgot was that once his father, too, could see."

Then, as if he had finished the story, Jacob stopped speaking and simply looked at the fire. The children turned to Jacob, showing disappointment at how the story had ended.

"Is that it?" said the girl. "We thought you were going to tell us a story about a giant."

"But I did," said Jacob, smiling, watching how silence invited expectation. "I told you a story about a boy who could have been a giant."

"How?" squealed the children.

"A giant," said Jacob, "is anyone who remembers we are all sitting on someone else's shoulders."

"And what does it make us if we don't remember?" asked the boy.

"A burden," answered Jacob.

I believe this is a parable for our times. For it not only reminds us of our debt to those who have gone before us, it challenges us to become the shoulders for the next generation. *Empower Your Kids To Be Adults* will help us stand strong, stand tall, and stand together. May we faithfully and joyfully accept the challenge.

Dr. Steve Moore, Vice President for Student Life
Baylor University, Waco, Texas

# Introduction

# Can We Abolish Adolescence?

Americans love being sophisticated, modern. So we bought into school consolidations. We piled our kids into ever bigger and better schools. At about the same time, we demanded that schools be free of discipline. Second graders threatened teachers not to touch them or their fathers would sue. The United States Supreme Court destabilized the cultural foundations by two decisions, (1) abortion on demand cannot be denied to any woman of any age at any time, and (2) "separation of church and state" was invented as a substitute for the founders' intention that there should never be an "established church" in this country. These two decisions contributed to our present teen crises: one devalued all human life and established a logical basis for teen suicide, which soon rose to become the second most frequent cause of death for teens. The other ripped all core values out of the schools: no Judeo-Christian and Islamic grounding in the moral code expressed in the Ten Commandments, and prayer was forbidden.

Soon students were holding their parents hostage for bigger and better symbols of being "in" with peers. School parking lots looked like the best used car lot in town—full of late model, fully-equipped sport utility vehicles and import sports cars. Teachers with integrity left the profession by the thousands. These kids were initiating themselves into the softest, highest consumption culture in the world—American adolescence! But some of us who are parents and grandparents, ministers, and other mentors of the young are waking up.

And we are ready to declare that perpetual adolescence as an emerging sub-culture has got to go. Children want to become adults. Parents are the original role models for their children and have enormous influence—unless and until their kids become card-carrying adolescents.

Then came the Littleton, Colorado, massacre on April 20, 1999, a terrorist rampage: Eric Harris and Dylan Klebold, a pair of Gothic cult killers, executed 12 fellow high school students and a coach, then turned their weapons on themselves—a total of 15 dead in the school. Another 24 were treated in several hospitals in Littleton, Denver, and other suburbs. The dead included ethnic minorities, athletes, and Christians—deliberately identified and taunted as they were killed. Cassie Bernall, age 17, responded when one of the gunmen cried out, "Anybody here believe in God?" "I believe in Jesus!" she said. They blew her away. After lacing Columbine High School with hidden bombs and spending ammunition in gunfire calculated to kill up to 500 of their school-mates, these poor little rich boys kept their suicide pact. Their late model import sports cars, also wired to blow up, remained in the school parking lot. Eric and Dylan shot themselves.

On May 31, 1999, in the wake of the April massacre at Columbine High School in Littleton, Lance Morrow in a *TIME* essay, page 110, comments on the current tragic situation and our failure to launch teens as adults:

> Humans…have turned the long stretch from puberty to autonomy into a suspended state of simultaneous overindulgence and neglect. American adolescence tends to be disconnected from the adult world and from the functioning expectation (the hope, the obligation) of entering that world and assuming a responsible place there. The word adolescence means, literally, growing up. There is no growing up if there is nothing to grow up to. Without adult connection, adolescence becomes a neverland, a Mall of Lost Children.

The positive response to this Littleton tragedy was predictable. The "remnant" of believing teens rose to the occasion during the terrorist attack, leading prayer huddles under tables, in an isolated greenhouse where one classroom emptied to put distance between themselves and the mad gunmen. Many of the funerals were marked by remarkable maturity, by original songs created by teens for the occasion of their friends' murders, and by the triumph of God's good. Dozens of teens who lacked Cassie's courage to own her walk with Jesus, have dug new depth in their walk with God as a result of the litmus test of potential martyrdom.

## Time to reflect?

I have been working with other people's children since I was 19. That makes more than five decades of intentional program development, ministry, consultation, and praying for and with teens and their parents. I was ordained, married, pastoring a church, and leading youth ministry adventures involving kids from churches in Kansas and Nebraska, all before I was 21. Now my wife Robbie and I are great-grandparents. This means our six grandchildren are all grand-adults now! Some things have changed profoundly since the middle of the twentieth century in mid-America. Then, most high school kids were already adults and had a solid connection to the life they were embracing beyond high school. I knew few who were grinding out a "high consumption, bankrupt your parents, and blow away anybody who gets in your way" kind of existence. Today the spin doctors label each new ten- or twenty-year group and give them grim names to denote their preoccupation with distancing themselves from everybody else and hanging on to their generation's insecurities and grievances.

## Empower Your Teens—To Be Adults!

This book is my primer for parents, ministers, and other mentors who care about teens in our culture today. I've arranged the flow of the book to walk you slowly through the challenges we are facing with our young. I raise the question "Will Our Children Become Human?" and ask you then to "Face Your Competition" as agents who empower and define your kids' worth and destiny. To help you see how your children are torn among competing value systems, I've then described "Your Kids and Their 'Systems'" on the way to finally defining "What Has Gone Wrong with Our Culture?" Then I invite you to walk around the central question of our time: "Who Invented Adolescence?" and beg you to join me in "Upstaging Adolescence: How Everybody Wins!" On the downhill slope and full of hope and strategies that work, I ask you to reflect with me on "Seeing the 'Image of God' in Your Kids," and recruit you to become a parent who consistently is "Empowering with Family Promises." Then I round out the book in a concluding chapter with examples of "Initiating Kids Through Community Rites."

It is clear that our young deserve the full attention of parents, ministers, and other mentors. Not every "village can raise a child," especially if the village is sick and lacks appropriate commitment to the vitality and maturing of its young. But it is true that families deserve support communities of faith and nurture to join them in the challenge of launching kids in a world that has essentially sold its children to the slavery of perpetual adolescence.

## Special Thanks!

Dr. Don Ratcliff of Toccoa Falls College in Georgia is a co-conspirator with me on many fronts. When he learned of the *Empower Your Kids* manuscript project, he wanted a pre-publication manuscript for his students to read in the spring of 1999 for EDU 243, Child Development. In the end Don arranged to place the whole book on the Internet. There his students could access it, read it, and respond to it. His students wrote thousands of paragraphs of interaction with the content and Don forwarded them all to me. So my final revision of this book is profoundly in debt to Don and the students at Toccoa Falls College who participated in this process. My own doctoral students from CE 815 Faith Development in the Family responded to it in their doctoral seminar in January 1999. Then, in the spring, my ExL distance learning students responded to it in CE 628 Developmental Issues in the Family. All of these students turned to the Internet website to read and respond to their challenges for their courses. All of them gave me direct interaction with the issues as we processed the analysis and strategies for upstaging adolescence. I refined the project substantially because of those gifts of interaction. So here it is—for all who are committed to turning children into adults through sharing the authority and passing on the best resources we have ever discovered.

# 1

# Will Our Children Become Adults?

Jim was restless much of his first year of graduate school with us. Near the end of the spring semester he told me he had a job for the summer with a college friend who was now married and doing well as a construction contractor. Jim was now twenty-eight, had taught school for four years out of college, then chose seminary to pursue some form of ministry.

"What then, after that?"

"Well, I think I'll just go home and live with my parents, pay off some college loans, and see what turns up."

"You can't go home again, Jim," I found myself saying. I had two sons whose ages bracketed Jim's age of twenty-eight. I could not imagine the pain of seeing one of my sons facing thirty and not knowing who he was or where his energy was needed in the world.

What are young adults up to in our culture? Not all are paralyzed at twenty-eight. Many are card-carrying adolescents—indulging in a career of irresponsibility and risk. We do spring break at New Smyrna Beach, just twenty miles south of Daytona Beach in Florida. While there we read the Daytona newspapers and watch Daytona TV news. A footnote to parents' anguish about full-grown adult children blasted us wide-awake. Daytona automatic teller machines reported dispensing millions of dollars every week to university beach bums living in expensive hotels. I had to lay the paper down and go for a swim. These poor, lost, extravagant adult children of theirs are obviously holding parents hostage, and parents are footing the bill for the extravagant consumption not only on spring break, but until—*Pray the day will come!*—these full-grown incompetents leave home, marry, and get a job. Some parents evidently support the fifteen year "fling" of adolescence out of regret that they didn't get to sow their wild oats. Others are simply supporting public extravagance for their kids that matches their past wasted years continued now as parents.

## It Takes Some Help to Launch a Kid!

We brought two sons from conception up through early manhood and celebrated, then and now, their magnificent embrace of adult skills and responsibility as they launched into productive and effective lives well out of the nest. Today they are our adult peers in most ways, and we are watching the next generation—their own children—embrace careers as adult women and men. These days they are giving us the "fourth estate," our great-grandchildren.

We did not launch them alone, of course. We had mentored other people's kids during a decade—the 60s!—of volunteer ministry with senior high teens in our church. I remember thanking one of those former group members for being there for Mike, our young son. I had seen the midweek Kid's Club group leader through some pretty tough sledding during his high school years. So he caught my direct reciprocal thanks when I said, "I enjoyed being there for you. I've been praying for a long time that somebody would be there for my sons. Thanks for keeping an eye on Mike."

It was Jay and Vicki Benson, a young married couple volunteering to coach Bible quizzing for teens in our church, who came through for John. They coached him and awakened his desire to go for the gold in district, state, and national championships. We had been there for Jay and Vicki, and cheered them on to develop their gifts and embrace their potential during high school.

This cooperative, joint support has a powerful magic in it: Parents are unconditionally committed to rearing their children and long to see them take wings and join them in the fulfilling destiny of adult career and family life. And the whole community cheers our young, wanting to bless and encourage them to be all that they can be. Ministers and other mentors of our young occupy special leverage positions. They literally become the "high priests" of adult initiation for our kids. It is urgent to have parental belief and support if you are a kid, but if you are to be taken seriously as an adult in the outside world, it requires outside guides and mentors to preside over your "graduation" into adulthood.

## Parents, Ministers, and Other Mentors?

This book is focused on this cooperative team of parents, ministers, and other mentors of our young. The main track will be for parents, but there are parallel guidelines laced throughout, to coach and encourage those community leverage folks who join parents in blessing and empowering their kids.

*Parents* are the birth or adopting or foster-caring adults who accept the challenge of providing abundant and long-term basic care, teaching, and shaping discipline. Parents welcome children into the human race. Robert Bly observes that a parent is basically charged with the challenge of keeping kids alive until they are grown.[1] But parents also know their best gift to the world is to make every effort to bring up a healthy, well-ordered, and productive human being. Add the spiritual core values to the billions of curricular teachings—words, behavior, attitudes, and beliefs—and all of us acknowledge that the parenting job is the wonderful and awesomely powerful leverage on the kid.

By *ministers* I want to support those who by volunteer or intentional vocation have chosen to invest in children and emerging young adults. Many of these volunteers are single, yet out of gratitude that people were there for them, they are investing in the next generation. Many of these volunteers are openly searching for a life vocation—a means of investing career energy in working for and with people. Often a minister is also a mentor. Sometimes the minister is also a parent, and will celebrate the signs that family members are receiving the magic of mentoring from someone outside the family. "We invested in other people's kids," Robbie and I sometimes reflected as our sons hit full height. "Who will be there for our sons?"

*Ministers* include people who see their life mission as "serving" the child. We have organized our seminary curriculum around a dozen courses with names which begin, "The Servant as...."[2] Typically, youth ministers, pastors, and other ordained people offer our kids visible models and style of mature adulthood. Link this visibility and credibility with the luxury of their careers as paid "Levites" in the oldest clergy tradition, and you will join me in thanking

---

[1]See *A Gathering of Men*, a PBS broadcast, 1990, New York: Mystic Fire Video. Bill Moyers interviews poet and men's advocate Robert Bly. Especially useful is Bly's description of every young man needing not only to be well-fathered, but later to find a mentor.

[2]At Asbury Theological Seminary, the core curriculum in the Master of Divinity degree revolves around a series of courses across the various disciplines, each titled, "The Servant as..."

God that there are men and women who have answered God's call to be career ministers and available to our kids. But many *ministers* are volunteers. Technically, ordination to ministry consists of baptism or other initiation rites to the Christian community. So my encouragement for *ministers* goes beyond ordained clergy and includes volunteers, teachers, directors, wranglers, small group leaders—any of those hosts of roles in which dedicated people serve in the name of Jesus.

*Mentors* have the luxury of picking up the easy part of the launching. Mentors come in all ages, both genders, and an older child or teen may be your kid's most influential early mentor. If college and university students hold middle school and high school kids in contempt, they miss a great mentoring potential. A *mentor* comes on line with your child in one of two ways: (1) The kid "nominates" the mentor by visible signs of admiration. Often these are unconscious positive signals of voice or face, or actual spoken words of high respect. (2) The mentor sees something to admire in a kid, perhaps potential missed by others including the family. Here the mentor shows signs of respect, a sort of invitation to conspire with the kid to make a good investment of his life and energy. Sometimes, of course, the signs and signals and words are reciprocal: the protégé and mentor simply "hit it off" in a unique way, and both know it is going to be a good journey. But mentors, unlike parents, have only a temporary job.

A *mentor* and a *protégé* work best together if they both accept that time is limited for their conspiracy to get the kid ready for launching and adult competency. If a *skill* is involved, the coaching season is predictably short. If a *life mission* is involved, we may be looking at a decade or more. Only rarely does a *mentor-protégé* relationship turn into a career partnership. Healthy *mentors* know when to launch and bless and accept the graduation of the *protégé* into full-speed ahead with career and adult life. Most of us move through a series of *mentor* relationships as we accept the models we adore, crack the mystery of their power, and adopt strategies and ways of working and being more effective in the human adventure. *Mentors* typically are a half-generation or more older than the *protégé*. And it is always the wisdom, authority, and responsibility of the mentor that attracts and holds the protégé.[3]

---

[3]See Bob Shank, *Enhancing Your Ministry Through Mentoring.* Pasadena: Charles E. Fuller Institute, Tape #2660, 1993. See also Eugene L. Peterson, *Working the Angles: The Shape of Pastoral Integrity,* especially part three, on spiritual direction, including getting a spiritual director and being a spiritual director. My own *Following Close: A Mentor in Your Life* is an audio tape seminar from a men's event in Nashville, February 1995, available from the author.

Wise parents, ministers and other mentors share one common vision of the kid: All of us know that we are fulfilled when the child is up and competent and ready to fly as an adult. I suspect we get our satisfaction out of watching the success because we were so well served by parents, ministers, and other mentors in our own time. The main job of a kid is to grow up. It is easy to believe that these parents, ministers, and other mentors were supposed to do their job—with very little thanks. The excerpt below of the Hensley/Silber masterpiece reminds us of how much we depended on people we admired, sometimes without full appreciation for their sacrifice:

> *I was the one with all the glory.*
> *You were the one with all the strength—*
> *Only a face without a name.*
> *I never once heard you complain.*
> *Did you even know that you're my hero?*
> *And everything I'd like to be?*
> *I can fly higher than an eagle,*
> *But you are the wind beneath my wings!*[4]

## Jesus: Parents, Ministers, and Other Mentors—a Case

Look at the amazing child-to-adult episode from the life of Jesus as we find it at the end of Luke 2, if you want to see the roles of parents, ministers, and mentors. We think of the account as reporting "The Boy Jesus Lost in the Temple." But note these amazing "community" partnerships in getting Jesus "launched" into his mission.

1. Jesus was fascinated with the Temple elders (the ordained ones) and the teachers (other lay ministers). He missed his signals to join the caravan leaving for home. The *protégé* caught sight of the *mentors* and was energized and spellbound listening to them and answering their questions.

2. After three days Jesus' *parents* found him. The Luke text says they were "astonished" when they saw him. The word specifically denotes emotional displeasure. They intended to see him live to grow up, and when he missed the caravan he was in a high risk situation, quite apart from the inconvenience of his parents losing most of a week out of their lives going after him.

---

[4]See the lyrics of "Wind Beneath My Wings," 1981, from the movie *Beaches.* The song is by Larry Henley and Jess Silber. Miami: Warner Brothers Gold Corp/Warner House of Music, at 15800 NW 48th Avenue, Miami, Fl 33014.

3. The Temple elders and teachers were "amazed" at Jesus' understanding and his questions. This specific word denotes highest admiration, even the wish "to have a child like this." This is classic *mentor* perception of a *protégé*. Mary and Joseph knew they had a special kid on their hands, but they were doing the essential parenting supervision. Jesus deserved to have outside, objective, and "neutral ground" *mentors* to give him feedback on his own gifts and potentials.

4. Jesus saw his destiny and even announced it to his parents as a part of his response to their reprimand. "Did you not know I had to be about my Father's business?" Mary wisely reflected on that one and likely matched it up with earlier unusual signs of Jesus' special destiny. So, in this one amazing story from a "rite of passage" event in Jesus' life, we can see this team of parents, ministers, and other mentors who play crucial parts in launching Jesus into his career and destiny as Savior.[5]

## Parenting Is Life's Best Job

Like you, we did most of our parenting in sort of unconscious states ranging from ecstasy to exhaustion. Overall, the years were good and the memories are heartwarming.

John, our firstborn, stretched every muscle to "be a man." One treasured color photo from his second year of life has him sliding around the house in my shoes—waddling like a man with oversized snowshoes.

Mike, our secondborn, at age six aroused both our adrenaline and our endorphins in an early morning school departure accident. We heard one of those sibling rivalry scuffles at the front door and the sound of the large storm sash breaking. His hand had gone through the glass and he shrieked as he saw the blood from a four-inch surface gash in his arm. There was nothing so trivial on his mind as blaming John for making him break the glass. Instead it was a primal wail: "Will I die? I want to grow up to be a daddy!" A quick trip to the emergency room and a butterfly bandage had him in his first grade classroom before the first hour of his school day had passed.

We are more alert to magic moments with our grandchildren. I suspect that our basic parenting years left us with too few memories for a couple of reasons. No doubt we were doing a pretty good job at daily empowerment of

---

[5]See my "Facing Stress in the Family," *Alumni Advance.* Wilmore, KY: Asbury Theological Seminary, pp. 12-15, Fall, 1990.

those two sons of ours, but we came up short on a couple of things: (1) We had no idea the years would whiz past so quickly and our basic parenting would be over. We think we were like most parents—operating out of spontaneous automatic pilot intuition or out of desperation and fatigue—determined to do a good job with our kids. We suspect that we often worked too hard, especially with our firstborn. And with both boys, we have some regrets that we failed to seize the moment for best learning with these irretrievable days of childhood.

But we think we see another simple deficit. (2) We had no adequate vocabulary to describe what we wanted to achieve as a result of our parenting investment with our kids. Benjamin Whorf gets the credit for observing that humans who have no words to describe common experiences have no tools for thinking about what they are doing.[6] Such linguistically-impoverished people, Whorf observes, will never break through to high achievement— simply because of a lack of words to describe what they want. At a much simpler level, for example, folks who have no names to distinguish among various species of flowers or birds are much less likely to pay attention to all birds and flowers than folks who have discovered names which denote distinction among the species. Here, I want to offer some vocabulary for describing the important developmental opportunities with our kids. I wish I had known the difference between a *parent* and a *mentor* before our children were out of diapers.

What I offer you in *Empower Your Kids* may help you with both of those deficiencies of my own basic parenting years. So if you are a parent, let me encourage you to celebrate the gift of the parenting relationship and the early years with your soon-to-be-adult kid. And think through the terms *parents, ministers, and other mentors*, and celebrate the important contribution each of them can make to your child's maturing. Here (1) I want to bless you and help you celebrate the small daily episodes of effective empowering you do with your kids. I want also to invite you to resolve to get very intentional about daily, as well as major, life-launching events of empowerment for your kids. And (2) I'm offering you some basic and pretty simple language for thinking about empowering and launching kids through family and community events. If you can get on board with these ideas, you can be sure that your kids will find mere adolescent partying looking pretty pale by comparison.

---

[6]It was Benjamin Whorf at Massachusetts Institute of Technology who observed what has now become "the Whorfian Hypothesis." It notes that a people is capable of achievements only for which they have a conceptual foundation in language: without words, there is no potential for thought.

I'm also asking ministers and other community mentors to look at the outsider's unique position of blessing, coaching, and celebrating your children across their lifetimes, but especially during the critical school years. We thank God for pastors, youth ministers, teachers in the schools and in the church, coaches, and choir directors for the ways they defined our sons' worth and energized them. John and Mike easily believed that there is life after childhood—and it is not a twenty-year "bash" of extravagant irresponsibility and consumption of scarce wealth. So I want these ministers and other mentors to look at all of the internal parenting agendas, and to accept that they have the luxury of harvesting the good planting which parents have done by birthing and parenting their kids so well. And in those cases where parents have disappeared or been unable to meet basic parenting needs, ministers and mentors often help to compensate for the losses and effectively launch solid young adults with only minimal contact and blessing.

You will find that what I say here is based on my belief that both parents and other mentors for our young are full of motivations they can trust when it comes to recognizing what kids need. I've dipped into memory to give you a couple of our own stories from the early years with John and Mike. So in every chapter, give yourself a chance to relax and dip into your own memories and stories from your own parenting experience. Make notes in the margin to remind you again and again about wonderful, funny, and other positive episodes in which you, too, were caught doing the right things as you empowered your kids. There you were—holding out to them gracious invitations to enter into the high country of fully human, fully alive adult pleasure and responsibility.

## Seize the Moment

I am more reflective as a grandfather, less anxious than I was as a father. And I have deliberately cultivated a "kid watching" vocabulary which helps me celebrate and appreciate what I am seeing as six grandchildren embrace their adult sovereignty before my very eyes. Imagine the pleasure of watching as their children arrive to guarantee "the fourth generation."

Some twenty-five years ago when Jason was under the age of two, I discovered I had naively tantalized him into joining me in a manly conspiracy. Jason is John's firstborn and our first grandchild. I spontaneously and inadvertently coached him through a powerful "delay of gratification" test. At that time I saw Jason's interactions with me in terms of simple pleasure. Not until later did I realize that these toddler-Grandpa exchanges were classic conscience development moments. We were building conscience through the interruption of anticipated pleasure, followed by the reward when prerequisite conditions had been met. Furthermore, I now realize I accidentally set up a complete "rite of passage" set of tasks. When I looked at anthropological and cultural rites of passage and examined the rite of passage model common to every tribal culture in the history of the human species, I was startled to see that the model fits almost perfectly over, and explains the power of, the episode with Jason.[7] Here's the account of my memorable exchange with Jason.

In May before Jason turned two in July, his parents were locked into a Marriage Enrichment weekend led by David and Helen Seamands. We were in Nashville with my "curriculum development" students visiting the Board of Discipleship offices for their orientation into instructional resources. So John and Julie dropped Jason off overnight with Robbie's parents—his great grandparents. They all promised Jason that "tomorrow, Papaw and Mamaw will pick you up for the weekend." In his early years Jason was an overnight guest at our house one or two Friday nights each month as we gave his young parents a night off from parenting, so the prospect of being with us evidently sounded appealing to Jason.

That sets the scene in which my invitation to a "manly conspiracy" unfolded. Robbie and I arrived from Nashville in early afternoon. It was a warm spring Saturday. When we rang the doorbell of the Bowles home, Jason scampered out to the porch and began pulling on my trouser leg, begging to go in "Papaw's big car." Jason's appeal was incessant. He was oblivious to the adult conversations that were underway, but he saw to it that I could not completely ignore him. To ease the annoyance of the pants leg appeal, I lifted him and cuddled him close in my spontaneous Grandpa hug.

We had intentionally skipped lunch, having gorged in Nashville on Friday and again at breakfast. But Mom Bowles insisted that we sample her new pound cake garnished with a scoop of ice cream. It was easy to yield to the temptation, so I explained to Jason that we were taking Mom's invitation.

"We're going to have some cake and ice cream, then we'll go in Papaw's big car." Jason accepted the delay. He had recently had lunch with the great-

---

[7]Move into chapter 2 for a glimpse of the "rites of passage" diagram I mention here. I have adapted it from A.H. Mathias Zahniser, "Ritual Process and Christian Discipline." *Missiology: An International Review*, Vol. XIX, No. 1, January 1991, Wilmore, KY 40390.

grandparents at the table where I was now sitting down. He busied himself around the kitchen where we were beginning to eat and visit with Robbie's parents. Shortly after my cake was served, I realized Jason had managed to crawl into my lap. I recall adjusting the chair to include this added depth. And I experienced the slight inconvenience of eating with a full head of baby hair brushing my own face as I tried to deal with finishing my cake and ice cream. Jason was not participating in the conversation or making any demands. I was hoisting each bite of cake and ice cream over his head as he, I thought, was facing the table to observe the other three adult occupants.

But as the final bite of cake left the plate, and before it reached my mouth, Jason's tiny 22-month-old hands reached out and seized the plate, pushing it as far toward the center of the table as he could reach. He announced calmly but with visible endorphin-stimulated urgency: "Now! Go in Papaw's big car!"

I scooped up the little tiger and returned the volley: "You're right. We're ready to go in Papaw's big car." We did our rituals of departure with Mom and Dad Bowles and found ourselves three-abreast in the front seat, Jason perched in his special seat.

## Second Ritual, Same Model

As I reconstruct the way the next five minutes unfolded, I am dumbfounded to realize that I repeated the whole tantalizing sequence with Jason one more time. In that second scenario I began to craft a conspiracy that involved the magical world of outdoor manly work and inviting him into my world of machines and lawn and sky. Jason was delighted to have won the privileges of riding high in Papaw's big car and to be on the way to Mamaw's house. In those pre-seat belt years, toddlers could ride where they pleased.

As we started the journey of about a mile toward our home, I savored the beautiful spring day. I fused that happiness with the comfortable feeling of grandfatherly affection for this first and only grandchild. Then I turned my good feelings into speech and simply rambled aloud to Jason what I wanted and needed to be doing on this lovely Saturday afternoon at home:

"Jason, do you know what we are going to do when we get to Mamaw's house? We're going to get out the lawn mower and the garden tractor and we're gong to work outside this afternoon."

Now, at 22 months, Jason would never have been allowed close to motorized lawn and garden equipment. And his healthy fear of my tractor and mower was, at that point, amazing to behold. While he liked the idea of manly use of the equipment, he would turn and run when I started the motor on either one. My invitation to join me in the work had such a powerful appeal to him that he bucked up and down in his car seat with visible excitement. (Only last week Jason's 10-month-old son, Caleb, re-enacted the same kinds of manly work alongside me and sometimes under my feet, grasping for my pitchfork or shovel to do the work himself!)

Minutes later, stopped in our circle drive to unload our weekend gear, I lifted Jason over me and stood him on his feet on the asphalt. Robbie and I were busy collecting our belongings for the trip into the house. I was quite unaware of Jason's excited romp to our equipment shed. But as I lugged the gear toward our back door, I heard his voice from the storage barn door about thirty yards away:

"Papaw! Tractor! Lawn Mower!" Verbs and power appeal phrases were not yet in his arsenal of words.

"Jason, look at me," I said. "I have to put these things away and change my clothes before I can work in the yard." Then, as an afterthought, I remembered something I had noticed as he sat on my lap at the table: "Besides, you're wet," I said. "Let's get you a dry diaper before we go to work."

I gave him no command, only established an agenda of prerequisites to the delightful task—things to be hurdled before he was eligible for this partnership in adult adventure in outdoor manly work.

My memory of the next few minutes is a blur of routine dispatching of clothes to the hamper or to the closet, of hanging up my travel clothes and slipping into my outdoor farm coveralls. But over my shoulder, I detected Jason's presence. This young man of 22 months was lying silently, patiently, spreadeagled on the floor, exactly on the throw rug in front of the commode. He had been there a hundred times before by adult demand, normally with resistance at interrupting his childhood agenda. In this prized moment, Jason was now presenting himself voluntarily, knowing that a dry diaper was the final requirement to which he must surrender if he would be permitted to work alongside Grandpa today.

I was dressed. In a flash he was clean and dry. Then with a fresh diaper installed, he stood literally jumping up and down with the excitement of the tasks ahead.

With a thumb and forefinger I lifted my hairpiece and placed it on a block in the sink cabinet. When I slapped my work cap in place, I offered Jason a small version of my own striped denim cap, which he liked to wear for manly work outdoors with me. But he grasped his blond forelock and yanked it upward.

"Jason…hair off!" He appealed to me matter-of-factly.

"I think it would hurt if you took your hair off."

"When I'm Papaw, Jason do it," he announced, installing his cap, as if there still remained that manly status of baldness yet to achieve—a grandpa hurdle separating him from the ultimate necessary manly proof: removing your hair as you go to work outdoors! We were out the door and off to the storage barn, but I had a good deal to think about from that exchange with my young grandson. With any genetic luck, he may not go bald. He enjoys one other visible line of genes in which men keep their hair.

## Catch Yourself Empowering Your Kids

Look at the ordinary day-after-day curriculum parents and kids are inevitably inventing—a curriculum with one single goal which is wonderfully both yours and theirs. But look at these simple stories from infancy and see them as a parable for ministers and other community mentors: children will adore you, imitate you, and want to *be who you are*. This is the absolutely irresistible magnet that works between a protégé and a mentor. Look at what parents and mentors have going for us:

*Kids want to be competent adults.* Every child wants to be what the parent is and do what the parent does from the first breath and the first gaze into parents' eyes. The adult world looks ideal, wonderful, the place to be, and so every waking moment the child is watching for clues about how to crack the code and to get into the adult world. I will discuss with you in chapter 2 what has gone wrong in our culture that breaks this deep and original desire of every kid. I will make the case that the natural appetite of childhood is to believe that they can grow up and become exactly like you—an adult with all the fun of freedom, competency, and productive responsibility.

Humming away inside every child is the motor of this desire. The kid has an amazing "unilateral respect" lens. Looking through that lens, you are perfect, larger than life, and awesome. The kid longs to grow up to do what you do, be who you are! Your kids stomp around clumsily in your shoes or hats or gloves. We laugh, but it is serious business, feeling this yearning to be exactly like the bigger folks around. Parents don't have to be perfect to look perfect to little eyes. Parents who goof can apologize to a child and the parents will only be enhanced and more "god-like" to the child than before. You were already perfect, so now you are out of this world because of your tender honesty. Count on it. Jean Piaget observed this child fixation on parents as "unilateral respect" of awesome big people, matched inside the kid as "adult constraint" to meet the unspoken expectations of perfection in the child.[8] Since this hunger is universal, parenting is made easy, and children develop resilience as we occasionally must delay gratification of their needs or dreams.

*Our vision is for kids to become our friends as adults.* What do you want for your kids? Well, it is really pretty simple: You want them to grow up, to be competent to manage life well, and to leave home as settled and responsible human beings. Add your specific family and spiritual trademarks to embellish the core, but all healthy young parents know from first embrace that children are a gift for only a little while, then they will be full grown. We worry that they may grow tall physically without maturing morally and spiritually.

What do you want for yourself? This part of the vision is easy, too, if you are honest and healthy. You want to be effective with your sons and daughters, to try your hand at this one-shot opportunity of shaping and launching new human beings. And you want the satisfaction of seeing them engage adult life well, both because you have blessed the world in that child, and because you have left your own signature on the future. So, since your children already adore you, older brothers and sisters, and other significant adults, and since they long to be what you are and do what you do, the "teacher" side of the curriculum is easily yours. In that unspoken, informal contract between you and the child, you are offering a way of being and a set of things to do which look irresistibly attractive to the child. So seize the moment early and spin out the curriculum content to meet the kid's changing agendas along the way to launching a son or a daughter as an empowered adult.

Every minister and mentor thrives on the small idolatry a child or teen directs to them in the search for outside endorsement. And effective ministers and mentors coach the kids to "be all they can be," not to become carbon copies of the mentor.

*Dance the adult dance.* Watch for kids' signals that they want to work with you, to learn everything you know and to be everything that you are. Recognize

---

[8]Jean Piaget defines "unilateral respect" as the one-way respect a child has for an adult, and "adult constraint" as the feelings of inhibition and control the child feels because of contact with an adult. These are entirely "constructs" inside the child's meaning-making mind, and bear little connection with the adult's eligibility for respect or actual efforts to constrain the child. The phenomenon shows up in the adult years as a protégé is shaped by a mentor.

and bless your kid's yearnings for time and lessons alongside you. I hope you accept the opportunity, take the inconvenience, and bless your kid's hunger curriculum easily, spontaneously, and infallibly. It sometimes sounds like this: "Would you like to go with me?" Any errand, any annoying interruption requiring you to go for repairs, to go across town, or across the street to rescue someone else—all are magic moments to bless the kid by forming a partnership. It doesn't make any difference whether the kid is three months, three years, or fifteen. When the parent or a mentor opens a slice of adult life and responsibility, the kid feels the pull of an inner magnet. They yearn to know, to discover, to experience what adults experience.

*Name the prerequisites.* If you can't take the kids on this trip or make them partners right now in this adult adventure, explain when they can go and what they have to get done in order to be ready. If the only delay is related to a more urgent immediate priority, state it and make a deal: "Can we get your homework finished before we take off?" "Can you quickly straighten your room, then we'll go?" "Let's grab all the trash and garbage and do that job on the run as we get out of here!" This "delay of gratification" strategy is a powerful motor to drive both you and a kid through unpleasant chores. But if you ignore priority responsibility in the child's present world and spring the kid free to run with you to an adult exploration, you make a deadly mistake. Such parental indulgence sets in motion a kid's pattern of expecting reward without responsibility. You don't want to live in the world with a full-grown kid who has been parented in this way. Such kids tend to lack motivation or conscience to fulfill responsibilities, and expect always to be pampered everywhere. But when pleasure is attached to unpleasant duty, the reward provides the basis for life-long love of work, high motivation, and a willingness to always accept the drudgery side of any career or job.

The "warrior" in classical fairy tale and myth is always the person who can stick to duty because the reward which follows is worth giving out any energy required to get the task done. Your kid wants to become a warrior in this classical "do the work first" sense, so be sure to design the parent side of the curriculum to match the kid's yearnings. Then, off to the adult task conspiracy.[9]

---

[9]Robert Bly in his PBS responses to an interview with Bill Moyers, *A Gathering of Men*, and elsewhere, defines the warrior characteristic as a person's persistent focus on task before pleasure. The warrior concept in fairy tales is not so much one of violent combat potential as of this faithfulness in the line of duty.

Mentors and ministers and other adored outsiders do the kid a favor as they coach the "warrior" completion side of every recruit or protégé. Invitations to join the team, the youth group, or other adventure without first completing home and school responsibilities is a conspiracy to extend the carefree, irresponsible sort of adolescence that is killing off millions of kids and is sinking our whole civilization.

*Celebrate the adult adventure completed.* Since you are determined to bless the kid's interest, fan into a flame the glowing embers of their yearning for time with you and for discovering the secrets of the adult world of work and responsibility. Now, when the prerequisites are met, the waiting has been heroically endured, or the emergency job is done, when the partnership has been sealed by the kid's gift of being your partner—two-year-old, ten-year-old, or teen, no matter—then you make the appropriate gestures of affection: "high fives," handshakes, hugs, bumps to the shoulder, whatever your ritual is. The message is, "We were adults together on this one." Across the decades of this relationship, and eventually from your son or daughter back to you, this warm affirmation arouses the best of all brain chemicals to promote well-being. Adrenaline may have been pumped to fuel a sudden emergency or a fright occasioned along the way to completing a tough job. But endorphins trickle from the brain under conditions of high anticipation, high pleasure, and a general sense of "feeling better all over than anywhere else."[10] These remarkable chemicals give a natural high while at the same time boosting the effectiveness of the immune system. Thus they both prevent susceptibility to illnesses and promote healing and recovery from current disease. Pharmacies stock no medicine as positive as this natural chemical which arises from contact with a respected and fully trusted person.

---

[10]Adrenaline rushes give an excitement and especially fear-based elevation in energy. A person who experiences danger in the home on a regular basis arouses to a heightened sense of awareness knowing that it may be necessary to "fight" or "flee." Years of these heightened fear-based and chemically marked episodes often lead to an addiction to adrenaline. So when the person marries a non-alcoholic, for example, and only feels normal dealing with the episodic adrenaline-heightened episodes, the child of an alcoholic can create a "need" for these episodes. This frequently factors into a person's taking up drinking in order to make the spouse feel "normal." Addiction to raging, perpetual activity, and other bingeing can create another generational pattern of abnormalcy. Endorphin highs, on the other hand, are natural highs. The endorphins are brain chemicals released in episodes of positive emotion. Most commonly, endorphin rushes occur when positive circumstances produce laughter. Other positive experiences such as appropriate sexual intimacy can be so elevating that they leave chemical markers in memory as near "out of the body" experiences of ecstasy. Illicit and inappropriate sexual contact often leaves an adrenaline marker brought on by the risks involved in non-marital sex. These adrenaline-evoking episodes frequently lead to addiction and repetition of the high risk "high."

*Generalize to the kid's world.* Because you have seen your own child perform alongside you, you will speak with authority when you affirm that she or he can handle some solo task coming up. You have created a series of impressive exhibits to encourage this adult when peers or self-doubt eat away at the sense of value or confidence your kid deserves. In a parallel way, ministers and other mentors serve as midwives to "deliver" the kid to adulthood, and a key part is the endorsement you can give of affirming the mature performance of the young adult.

*Tell it on the mountain.* You will report to other adults about your child's competence and your pleasure at having had his assistance on the mission accomplished together. You will speak honestly, discreetly, but with visible pleasure. And you will speak in the presence of your child, who is enhanced at every telling of the truth about young competency, first at home, then to friends. Ministers and mentors find appropriate occasions to give both personal feedback and public acknowledgment that the young protégé is competent, productive, and moving ahead in grasping adult responsibilities.

## Unilateral Respect—Constraint Energy

Watch the ingredients which mix into the indelible and powerful motivation when the kid's desire and the parent's resources come into a magical connection:

> 5. **Parent or mentor guarantees delivery on schedule!**
>
> 4. **Kid and model both play by the rules, watch the clock and wait together.**
>
> 3. **Parent or mentor blesses kid's desire, and states any prerequisites.**
>
> 2. **Kid signals or states a strong desire which parent or mentor controls.**
>
> 1. **Kid is caught in the magic of unilateral respect for superhuman parent or mentor.**

Now revisit your own experience with this magical staircase formula. Christmas hopes and birthday expectations are annual times to strengthen the child's conscience and moral courage by waiting the countdown of the calendar. When children deeply want any object or experience, you have done

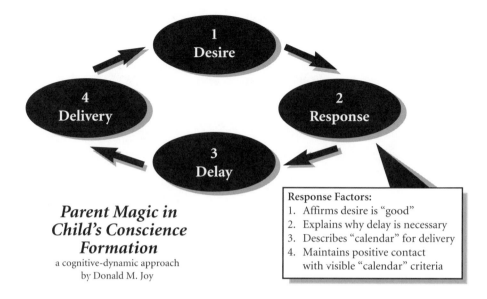

**Parent Magic in
Child's Conscience
Formation**
a cognitive-dynamic approach
by Donald M. Joy

**Response Factors:**
1. Affirms desire is "good"
2. Explains why delay is necessary
3. Describes "calendar" for delivery
4. Maintains positive contact
   with visible "calendar" criteria

them a favor to help them count the cost and look at the calendar, in relation to a time when they can get everything together to achieve the target.[11]

Consider the driver's license, the car to drive to special events or to school, and a dozen other marker events every kid wants to experience. When any of these targets is potentially constructive and reasonable for your child in its time, be sure to construct a time line to make maximum positive use of the child's desire and your role as coach and game master in this Olympic stretch for the gold, or responsible adult targeting. Mentors and ministers and other coaches of kids observe in every protégé the desire, the discipline of preparation and waiting, and the deserved embrace of one of life's most important trophies.

But we are likely to rob our children and to render them weak of conscience and moral integrity if we quickly supply their desires with no shared contemplation of the target while the full passion is driving their yearning.

---

[11]See my *Beyond Adolescence: Hope for Teens and Families*, an eight-session video teaching program available only from the Office of Continuing Education, Asbury Theological Seminary, Wilmore, KY 40390, or by phoning 1-800-2-ASBURY. These 1996 sessions include: The Mystery of Parent-Child Bonding, "Desire" and the Young Child, God's Curriculum for Children, Who Invented Adolescence, Creation Revisits Conception, Risk-Proofing Your Family, Cultivating Resiliency, and Let's Abolish Adolescence!

Nancy Gibbs reported on an experiment with four-year-old children and marshmallows.

> It turns out that a scientist can see the future by watching four-year-olds interact with a marshmallow. The researcher invites the children, one by one, into a plain room and begins the gentle torment. "You can have this marshmallow right now," he says. "But if you wait while I run an errand, you can have two marshmallows when I get back." And then he leaves.
>
> Some children grab the treat the minute he's out the door. Some last a few minutes before they give in. But others are determined to wait. They cover their eyes; they put their heads down; they sing to themselves; they try to play games or even fall asleep. When the teacher returns, he gives them their hard-earned marshmallows. And then, science waits for them to grow up.
>
> By the time the children reach high school, something remarkable has happened. A survey of parents and teachers found that those who as four-year-olds had the fortitude to hold out for the second marshmallow generally grew up to be better adjusted, more popular, adventurous, confident, and dependable teenagers. The children who gave in to temptation early on were more likely to be lonely, easily frustrated, and stubborn. They buckled under stress and shied away from challenges.[12]

Keep the diagram in mind and watch for lessons we can learn. Here are some of the easy ways to build with the strength of postponed fulfillment of children's desires:

1. Listen well to their articulation of the desired target and what they expect it will add to their personal satisfaction. Make it a rule never to mock the kid's target aspiration as impossible or foolish. Hear the kid out and allow the parent-child brooding to mellow the desire and refine the target without parental insult or shaming.

2. Join them in the anticipation. Endorse the target, even elevate the quality within reason—toward a better quality product for only slightly longer inconvenience or waiting, for example.

3. Invite the child to describe ways to meet the earliest possible target date, especially in describing what he can do or contribute to achieving the target and doing it in minimum time.

---

[12]Nancy Gibbs, "Marshmallows—The EQ Factor," reported in *Time* magazine, October 5, 1995. Cited by Joshua Harris in *I Kissed Dating Goodbye*. Sisters, Oregon, 1997, pages 80-81.

4. Keep your promises, including your part of the good conspiracy. Help kids focus anger toward any flaw that may appear while the waiting game is in progress. Eliminate the possibility that the child could think he was dumb, stupid, or that his desire was unworthy.

## Ritual Space and Rites of Passage

In chapter 2, "Face Your Competition," I will be offering you a vocabulary to extend this "interruption of desire for later delivery" kind of magic. I will offer a "rites of passage" diagram developed by my colleague, Professor Mathias Zahniser. It further unfolds how humans have been initiating their children into the world of adults for as long as we humans have been on this planet. Humans have such a long dependency that we have to get intentional about breaking our own parenting hold on the kids and about welcoming them into the world of adults. You will see ways to turn your major empowering events into events supported by your circle of friends and peers.

In this chapter, what I wanted you to sense is that both parenting and mentoring are rich roles for creating and blessing our coming generation of adult humans. Mostly it is as simple as accepting complicated but entirely spontaneous events which kids initiate with us as we assure them that they can, indeed, achieve their dream of becoming just like you—*Oh! Bless their innocent eyes!*—a superhuman adult with all the rights, responsibilities, and privileges that go with that adored status.

If you are engaged in honest enjoyment and partnership activities with your child, you are doing everything necessary. What we can predict is that you will move easily to the rites of passage which profoundly empower the kid to enter the world of adult freedom and responsibility, and your kid will be ready.

Imagine my pleasure at taking a phone call when Jason, that firstborn grandson of mine, phoned to ask if I would be in my office if he drove immediately the twenty miles to see me. I cleared an hour at once. Jason brought Becca to my office, partly to show me the diamond that became the marker to hold May 28 as a target for their wedding. But Jason also wanted to outline some of the financial planning they were doing to get both of them to Indiana Wesleyan University the next fall. He had begun his college academic and athletic career there in September. Together Jason and Becca had calculated their eligibility for scholarships and financial aid, and I celebrated all over again that he has been able to crack the secrets of the adult world. He had told me long before that he wanted to know everything I knew about being able to manage on a minister's and a professor's income and being able to be generous with so many people. Now I was in the luxury seat of watching Jason demonstrate his financial management skills right on schedule, and noting that at nineteen he was both competent and confident.

There is no question but that together this young bride and groom have asked the right questions and that they will find the solutions necessary to manage as adults in a very complicated world. That little tiger of a partner from infancy is now seizing full adult responsibility, and Jason and I are partners now in new ways. They married that May. Not long ago they surprised us during a holiday visit, as they often do.

"Are you guys still up? Could we come over?" Then, an hour later, after we had all chattered like magpies as we caught up with each other's experiences and hopes, when Jason sensed that their mission was accomplished, he stood, extended hands to Becca and to me, and looked at his Grandma.

"Can I pray with you before we go?"

We circled up as we've done so many times, and I almost melted down. *How could we get a grandson who would become the family "priest" in a moment like this?* I could not be more pleased as I celebrate the dignity, freedom and amazing skill with which Jason and Becca are engaging their vision of full adult responsibility.

# 2

# Face Your Competition

Our friends Harold and Verna worry that they are losing their son. They recently discovered that young Harry was smuggling skin magazines to his room. His mother found them when she was cleaning. And his musical tastes have shifted to what sounds pretty angry and rough to Harold and Verna. Harry mostly listens on his CD headset. They know his TV watching has turned to channels on their cable service that they find jarring just to skim across. And they have found that their home computer log traces his late night fascination with hits on pornographic websites.

What do you say to a kid who is caught in the grasp of electronic and print messages that scare you? Well, Harold and Verna brought the whole thing up with Harry at a late Saturday breakfast:

"Harry, can you tell us what the music channels and the movies you are watching are doing to you? Do you like how you are changing? We're worried about the print and web pornography you seem to be consuming. Do you really want to get hooked on electronic and print sex? Can you help us understand what is changing about you? We're really confused."

"It's this simple," Harry confessed. "I know the stuff is bad, OK? I know you are disappointed in me. And that hurts some. But this is my generation's stuff. Don't you get it? And even if it kills me, I'd rather be dead than not be doing what everybody else is doing. Can you understand that? I've got to be able to think about all of this stuff. I know you want me to sign up for this *True Love Waits* thing, but with what's going on in the real world I'm not ready to wear a chastity belt."

## Standoff with an Alien?

So, you feed the kids, clothe them, take them to Little League, soccer, and Sunday school. You teach your children to brush their teeth, take baths, to look and smell decent when they go out of the house for any destination.

And then the kid says, "No thanks! I've made a choice to be like folks who trim and brush their hair a different way. I want to be among those who look and smell alike." You could add a few lines: "And you are addicted to being among those who spend money but don't earn it. You constantly make extravagant demands on parents, but have no plans to be parents or to bless your own children with abundant food, clothing, and shelter or to take them to Little League, soccer, and Sunday school."

Do you get it? The power shifts with some kids, and they curse the hands that fed them. What makes it even harder is that they seem ready to bless the stars who seduce them. They lay down your money for tickets to stampede into an arena to worship heroes who inflame them to hate you. Furthermore, they seem to adore the very peers who abuse them and humiliate them. Your kids participate in blood rituals of initiation into a sub-culture which operates by one central belief:

> You'll be a stupid adult if you grow up.
>
> Hang on to your adolescent lifestyle.

This teen culture is being manipulated and fed by the electronic and print media, which greedily collects billions of dollars in advertising revenues and manufacturers' sales. That conspiracy is pulling our kids into a high-speed chase of satisfaction for their awakening appetites for significance, for community, and for love. For a chilling and detailed study of this lifelong adolescence virus now at work dismantling our culture, see Quentin Schultze and his colleagues from Calvin College, in their *Dancing in the Dark.*[1]

Never mind that fast-lane kids end up depressed, suicidal, and bedded down with lifelong viral diseases as direct effects of their obedience to the call of peer subculture hype. They are creating a lifestyle of extravagant consumption and hyperactivity that will predictably drive them as long as they live. Their new bumper sticker reads: *Forever Adolescent!*

---

[1]Quentin J. Schultze, et. al., *Dancing in the Dark: Youth, Popular Culture and the Electronic Media.* Grand Rapids: Eerdmans, 1991.

Your kids may never leave home, or may keep returning between fast-track misadventures. But their energies will always be sapped by nonproductive games, and you are likely to have to pay the bills for their continuing adolescent episodes of "living it up" well into their forties. They will need psychiatric help, many of them for years, and some will turn their addiction to the fast lane into an addiction for recovery groups, attending meetings almost daily in their shame-driven search for recovering significance, community, and love.

## What Everybody Needs

Since the first family settled down with a growing nest of children, every kid has been searching for a readable road map to adulthood. Not only was Harry looking up into the faces of our friends Harold and Verna because he was little and they were big. He was looking up into their faces because he started out his life adoring them as guardians and guides in the journey to adult maturing.

Our kids born to us when we were twenty-five become full-grown adults when we are forty. If we live to be seventy-five, that gives us thirty-five years to be peers and friends, blessed by fifteen years of our care and the child's dependent needs. That means that you could spend twice as long as adult peers of your kids as you spent raising and launching them. Get ready. Your own final fifteen years may be dependent, too—on your kids for decisions, baths, and other urgent needs. This book is totally focused on what everybody needs, and exploring ways of getting those needs met in ways that bless the kids, ourselves, and the whole planet.

## Getting from Here to There

If the universal kid hunger is to grow up and to be like the adults who cared for them, then we can narrow our search to look for universal patterns in the ways kids become adults. If we look carefully, we may discover that children turn into adults more effectively and productively in some cultures than in others. It is clear that youth violence, depression, suicide, and wasted energy plague North America at a very troublesome rate. Can we, by looking at history and at other present cultures, find a way to fix what has gone wrong here?

I have been trying to crack the code on adolescence since I was twenty, simply because I began to notice that many of my peers were being driven by crazy-making pressures that I found very silly when they tried to use them on me. My first attempt to put down my observations about adolescence appeared in a book in a chapter looking at "psycho-social development of adolescence."[2] I drew on cross-cultural studies and on more than twenty years of youth ministry. I had suffered shock and finally understood much of what I had observed in youth ministry as I studied with Professor Boyd McCandless, world authority on adolescence, in my doctoral work at Indiana University. Then, in his 1989 lecture to new graduate students here at Asbury Theological Seminary, my colleague A. H. Mathias Zahniser reported on rites of passage across cultures.[3] I took notes and began to expand my model of adolescence. The leap forward appeared in *Parents, Kids, and Sexual Integrity* in 1988, revised and re-released in 1993 as *Risk-Proofing Your Family.*[4]

Look at my slight adaptation of Professor Zahniser's diagram. Walk through it at least twice. First, trace your own journey from childhood to adult career and parenthood. Second, walk through the diagram again, asking how your children are going to walk this rugged road from childhood to becoming an acknowledged adult.

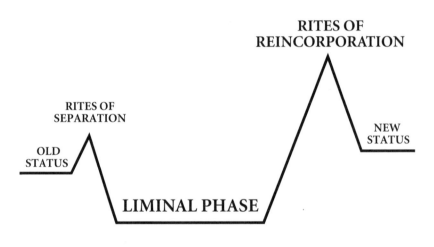

**RITE OF PASSAGE STRUCTURE**

[2]See my "Adolescents in Psycho-Social Perspective," in Roy B. Zuck and Warren S. Benson, eds., *Youth Education in the Church.* Chicago: Moody Press, 1968, revised 1978, pp. 91-105.

[3]Drawing is adapted from A.H. Mathias Zahniser, "Ritual Process and Christian Discipling." *Missiology: An International Review,* Vol. XIX, No. 1, January 1991, Wilmore, KY 40390.

[4]See my *Risk-Proofing Your Family,* Pasadena: U.S. Center for World Mission, William Carey Library, 1995, revised from my *Parents, Kids, and Sexual Integrity.* Waco: Word Books, 1988.

*Old status.* Let this represent "the world that was" of your childhood. Can you recall your sense of awe extended unilaterally toward parents and other significant adults? Awaken the sensations by which your magnet found the "adult target" and you saw your parents and mentors as magical and god-like people who were worthy of every imitation. Can you feel the helplessness, dependency, exposure, and vulnerability to them as parents met your basic needs, ranging from cleaning your ears to tying your shoes, to managing your schedule of childhood obligations, getting permission slips signed, and keeping you basically fed, warm, and comfortable? And your minister or other mentor knew your soul, your secrets and fears—especially those you feared disqualified you for respect in the adult domain. Think of your own transition from childhood to adult status.

*Rites of Separation.* What episode brought a sense of "elevation," of promise that childhood would soon be over? Recall the brief glimpse from a new peak experience that announced the end of childhood as usual.

*Liminal phase.* Now go back to the price you paid for awhile before you were a fully licensed, card-carrying adult. This liminal or threshold period tends to have a time clock or a calendar, a waiting period. Notice in the drawing that the status feels far below the peak of what was promised in the rites of separation. There you got a glimpse at adult powers and privileges. But you look back and say, "I was positively shaped by the liminal weeks or months or years. And entering into my sovereignty as an adult was well worth paying the price required to earn the right to enter in." How I hope your parents' promises of light at the end of the tunnel of adult desires served you well. And I hope there were ministers or other mentors who made credible that there is "life after childhood" and that the waiting and the deep longings were worth paying attention to. And if at twelve you chose to imitate a sixteen-year-old, I hope that emerging adult was truly adult, and not an arrested adolescent refusing the challenge of high responsibility.

*Rites of reincorporation.* Can you remember the celebration? How were you welcomed into distinctly adult status? This is the highest peak, better than settling down to adult life. I hope that somewhere it happened in ritual space: "Bring forth the best robe and put it on her, and place the family crest ring on her finger!" This highest, most rewarding ritual comes immediately after the waiting-paralyzed-through-the-dues-paying liminal phase. When the transition to adulthood goes well, there are emcees who host the peak celebration. They tend to be mentors or ministers or other respected adult coaches who have recognized your value and potential and have tutored and blessed you. They are the first to treat you with respect, even before the ritual time and space deliver the new status. They bless you by associating with you, naming you, and naming your journey worthwhile—lending you their personal authority. And they do it in the ears and/or the eyes of your soon-to-be new peers—the wider population of admired adults. Did you miss having your own rite of passage celebration? Was there no mentor as midwife?

*New status.* Childhood is forever behind you. "When I was a child" kinds of memories comfort you, knowing you will never go back again to the weakness, the powerlessness, and the dependency of your infancy and youth. You have been initiated. You likely have a new name. And you are being taken seriously. You will preside over the initiation of others who have stood the test of the liminal phase. You will state the new rules governing this Promised Land you've won. What images come to mind as you revisit your own investiture with adult status? How old were you? Who presided? Who were those most impressed with your worthiness to be elevated? Has it been a good domain since you embraced your full adult role, stature and responsibility?

## To Initiate or Not?

The late Joseph Campbell, sensitive philosopher that he was, is said to have observed once that "If we do not initiate our young into adulthood, then they will try to initiate each other."[5] I invite you to grieve over the youth chaos and tragedy of our times. Let Campbell's diagnosis motivate you to paint a better picture, to make a better offer to our young ones. They have gazed into our faces begging to be initiated into the wonderfully admired status of becoming *adults like us.*

Now, if you didn't do a stereophonic walk—your own history and your child's present alternatives—through the rugged path of the rites of passage, walk your kid through it now in your mind. Review the diagram by pulling the face of that wonderfully special teen into your imagination. Turning back to the Zahniser "Rites of Passage Structure" drawing, let your index finger do the walking and pause at each of the stages along the line. For each one, do a

---

[5]Joseph Campbell coined the phrase in a *Life* magazine excerpt from David Cohen, ed., *The Circle of Life: Rituals from the Human Family Album.* New York: HarperCollins, 1991. I had been saying virtually the same thing across three decades when I first noticed teens in our youth ministry in the 1960s were completely in awe of their peers. It was clear the teens would comply with any demand or performance in order to have the "badge of approval" which was an alternative to the blessings of family and significant other adults, since the adults were not a source of empowerment to them at that time.

worst-case scenario. Imagine the rituals that teen's peers are ready to perform as they try desperately, and often with deadly ritual, to change your kid into "somebody" with peer loyalty and peer status. They are offering a counterfeit of your offer of the true Promised Land of becoming the adult they were born to be. Let your well-informed mind predict how well your special teen person will be prepared to embrace all of life, to build solid and respect-based relationships in career, marriage, family, and the community after the peer rituals. If you yourself are in the college years, who are you mentoring who is still in middle school or high school? And how can you support the Promised Land of adulthood vision that is holding you steady, too? And if you are not mentoring a younger kid, then why are you not doing that? Is that a sign that you are postponing your own transforming journey as a young adult?

Finally, trace the line one more time, perhaps with your eyes closed. Let your imagination ignite with "best case" scenarios at each point. At some level this is your own prayer, and it is a cry to God to help you upstage counterfeit peer rewards and a life of permanent adolescence—the limbo of irresponsibility and extravagant consumption.

I said to Justin, my look-alike nineteen-year-old grandson, "You always have reminded me of myself. You've looked like me at any age I've seen you since you were born. If I ever seem to be enjoying you for no reason at all, you deserve to know the secret: I had a happy childhood and launching, and I want you to move through that transition well, too." You can be sure I want Justin to find empowerment right into his adult world without having to submit to the cruel and high-risk initiation rites of his peers. So many of his peers are starving for just a little promise from parents, ministers, and other mentors. They would give anything if some really trusted adults would pay any attention at all and would initiate them into the ultimate life secrets of the world of adults.

Enjoy that mental video you created. Mark it *Do Not Erase* and embellish it often as you re-run the images and contemplate the best of all possible rituals and circumstances that could come to your young and admired teens across the rites of passage structure.

In this chapter I have wanted you to face the competition out there which can destroy your kid in an effort to initiate and bestow peer significance. What sort of "adolescence monster" have we created in our culture? When we see the time line, it hasn't been around very long. Could we create a scenario in which illusionist David Copperfield could make it go away? Better yet, let's conspire to take back our kids and to haul out the real gold of the Promised

Land of adult privileges and responsibilities. We had the magic of their admiration during their infancy and early years. Believe it! We can get them back if parents, ministers, and other mentors begin naming the goals we have for the kids and we begin telling them the truth about our love and respect for them. If they know we are ready to bless them, they will trust us to deliver the goods of adult status, value, and responsibility.

We are clearly facing an enemy. It is not our children. The enemy is our culture. We have turned over our kids to overpopulated schools and expected them to find their own way through the war zone of adolescence into a productive adulthood. We have been pretty consumed just keeping them fed and clothed. Too often we have missed the cues that they want more from us— they want to know if they are going to ever be taken seriously. Can you imagine a scenario in which we attempted to make peace with our kids and to refocus our energy and theirs, taken back from a culture gone wrong? Perhaps then we could conspire with our own children to buy back the wasted years and create a new family system that reduces the risks and guarantees the future—one household, one block at a time.

In chapters that follow, I will walk with parents, ministers, and mentors showing you a supermarket of alternatives. From these, you can select and design strategies by which to empower and initiate your kids and welcome them to the "majority" of their lives.

# 3

# Your Kids and Their "Systems"

Mitch and Ron were the same age as our two sons. We lived only three miles apart. That put our kids in the same school environments from kindergarten through high school graduation.

Robbie and I chatted with their parents in chance meetings in the community. We kept current and watched comparisons and contrasts between our separate pairs of boys. Lorna mused over our plans for a weekend in Chicago:

"I don't know how you get your boys to go with you. Our guys won't go to Florida or anywhere with us. They'd rather stay at home or with their grandparents so they don't miss anything going on with their friends around here."

And across the street, we watched four healthy boys come up from early childhood, often playing in our backyard. In fact, I executed their haircuts for a few years as they lined up and begged for hairstyles just like our two sons. They adored their parents, wanted to be with them all the time. But we groaned a little inside to watch them left behind when the parents managed a special fishing trip once or twice each year. I think they were left behind because it cost too much to take six people away for a week. But the boys' hearts were with the grown-up activities.

And us? We practically lived our lives around schedules that had all four of us at recitals, football games, basketball, tennis, and choir concert tours. We sometimes rode as chaperones during the years our sons shaped up under the choral coaching of a miracle-working woman. But our sons were excited to pack and run with us to attend state or national conferences where Robbie or I were presenting or picking up professional training. Those sons of ours actually loved being uprooted to join us for summer courses at Indiana University while Robbie crammed her post-graduate reading specialist training and I leaped toward completion of the Ph.D. They spent endless hours indulging in "all day" rates at the campus bowling alley, and actually won Bloomington recreation tennis champion trophies as summer residents of Campus View and Tulip Tree apartments.

When our boys began dating for special events, every new friendship that turned into a date required a photo session and a stop off in early evening to pose in front of the Nikon, against the day the slides hit the wall to everybody's satisfaction. We celebrated the day when John and then Mike earned driver's licenses. We were wonderfully delivered from running a taxi service to rehearsals and athletic practices. But we were front row cheerleaders at all of their public events and followed our sons' children through both school events and recreational soccer, as well as championship swimming, and university level cross-country and track events.

We've watched the families whose children were friends of our own. And we have wondered whether some of the unusual breakdown in getting some of them effectively launched as productive adults may have been predicted by something toxic turned loose within the family relationships. We don't know whether the breakdown occurred in early childhood, or in something that separated them as pubescence hit. What we know now is that every family forms a powerful "system" in which each member plays out specific roles defined within the family—mostly hammered out behind closed doors at home. And every member of a family knows what is expected and how to maintain a balance. Any member's emergency or persistent need shifts everybody else's role. So a serious illness or "the affair" can so drain family energy that other members' basic needs do not get met very well.

What is true of every family is also true of each of the systems in which every person lives and moves. In every system, every participant has specific assignments of role, status, value, and responsibility. This is true in a family, a tribe, a school or workplace group, a community network, or recreation team. *A system consists of a group of people so "locked in" with each other that they automatically define who everybody is and how valuable they are to the group and how much power-authority-responsibility is entrusted to them.*[1] Here is the four-quadrant grid that includes most of our family ways of being together.

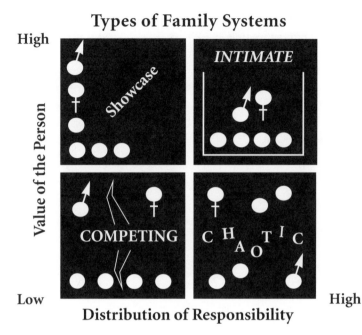

**Types of Family Systems**

Typical adults are locked into several systems: home, extended family, work or school, church, and other necessary or voluntary centers of affiliation. Many children live and move in multiple systems. This is obviously true with children of divorce who learn the rules and discover how they are valued in each of the households between which they shuttle. But children are enveloped in systems involving recreation, school, and church groups in which they experience role-status-value rewards. The four-quadrant drawing above can likely be spun to apply to any other system, since each of the quadrants predicts how members of the system are regarded within that system: High value of persons, or low? High distribution of responsibility, or none? If a

---

[1]See my *Risk Proofing Your Family* (Pasadena: U. S. Center for World Mission, the William Carey Library, publisher). Ralph Winter, founder and president, initiated conversations which led to the release of this 1995 title. Chapters 8 through 12 describe some basic family "systems" through which we may progress or bounce around in our search for effective relationships in our homes. The 4-quadrant "window" of systems drawn here stresses the importance of "high value" and "high distribution of responsibility" as keys to healthy family relationships. Phone the U. S. Center for World Mission at 800-647-7466 for information and ordering the book.

system is painful to us and pays off in humiliation, zero value and zero authority, we tend to escape those systems.

The only thing that holds people in painful systems is some desperate need to survive. Adults recognize survival needs as including retirement benefits, fringe protections such as medical and hospital insurance, or lack of an alternative place to escape and be enveloped in a safer and more rewarding system. Most people who take initiative in filing for divorce are in search of a more rewarding marital "system." And often their perception is clouded by the fog of Eros which distorts the vision of a potential system far beyond reality.

## You and Your Systems

Now that the family systems lens has been polished for us, we have taken repeated looks over our shoulders to try to see what we were doing with our own children, looked at "systemically." Since everybody lives and moves in several systems at the same time, our favorite system tends to be the one in which we find our greatest rewards of role, status, value and authority.

Look at your own systems now that you are a parent, a minister, or a mentor. This is a revealing reflection for all of us, but is especially useful to the emerging young youth ministry volunteer who is single, and is exploring the adult world in contrast to that of the American adolescent subculture.

When I compare (1) my marital system with (2) my family of origin system, (3) my father-mother-and two-sons system, (4) Grandpa-Grandma-six grandchildren system, (5) and my professor-author-speaker system, I can easily identify my most rewarding one. My marriage is my most supportive system, giving me the highest value, the highest attention and affirmation, and responsibility. But you will not be surprised that my Grandpa-Grandma-six grandkids-two great-grandsons-system is easily my second-most affirming system. And these grand- and great-grandchildren have almost no grasp of what I do as professor, author, and speaker. Do you have some idea why my sense of role, status, value, and responsibility are all so highly energized when I connect with those six grandchildren, now all adults, and with these first two from the "children's-children's-children" generation?

We have actively provided care for our grandchildren. We have "kidnapped them" in the early years for frequent overnight visits in our home—both to absorb precious time with these extensions into a new generation and to provide their busy parents with a honeymoon break from the high demands of their young children. Today we are flattered when a high-school grandson phones to say, "Grandpa, would you have time to keystroke in a paper I just finished? My teacher always likes it when it is printed on your laser printer and when the spelling has been checked. And the cover page you can make, you know. She really likes those too." Or a college sophomore phones from thirty miles away to say she has a rough draft done on a paper on child development, and could I get it in the computer, complete with footnotes and a bibliography? These kids think we can walk on water, and most of the time we can deliver what they need—a special costume located in our attic, or antique World War I helmet or London police helmets in our arsenal of hats with which they have played children's games. So we're delighted to have a young driver phone to say, "My folks aren't home tonight and I'm a little scared. Can I drive out and spend the night with you?" Is this a rewarding "system" for us? Can you see how our role, status, value, and responsibility have topped out completely off the charts with high reward for us?

Look now at basic systems in which your kids live and move. They include your own family of origin, their extended family, the community in which they move, and their "work" environment of school, clubs, and recreation contacts.

## System One: Your Household

Remember: Everybody lives and moves in multiple systems. And everybody is constantly evaluating how rewarding each system is and how to get more time and energy invested where the rewards are highest.

Everybody's primary system is the family. From conception up through the preschool years, most of us were aware of only one system: our family. We develop our sense of self-respect from readings we take in our primary family system:

| | |
|---|---|
| of role: | how we fit; what our "job" is in the system |
| of status: | how important we are to others |
| of value: | how we are affirmed and cherished |
| of responsibility: | what our contribution is to making things work around here, easily seen as the gift of authority or "empowering." |

You can see that what we call self-esteem is not really "self" bestowed at all. Check your own sense of self-respect. Ask how you arrived at the "sum total" judgment about your own value. Self-esteem or self-valuing is the gift of value placed on a person from outsiders: parents, the family system, specific mentor-peers, and the peer system. Together, these accumulated messages from all these outside "authorities" on how valuable you are add up to your sense of value or self-respect. And each system assigns a different role, status, value, and responsibility to you—matching your value and usefulness within that system.

Look at four factors your kid taps into in the search for identity and empowerment. If what is available at home leaves the kid feeling bankrupt compared to what other systems outside the family are offering, you will know your competition is in other systems, not in isolated people who can do harm to your kid.

*Value and Status.* You can see that families which give consistent readings of high value, and whose tutoring leads to the kid knowing how important a contribution he/she makes to the daily operating of the family—a matter of status in the family—is going to think tall, feel important, and be highly confident that the status and value hold true even beyond the home. Such a sense of value and status goes a long way to help anybody survive, even in demeaning and humiliating settings where some inescapable system grabs the kid for a semester's class or a summer's job. But if there is low value and no status sense in the family, the kid is going to be ready to listen to any peer-mentor—often "the voice of experience." Or the kid will pay attention to the peer culture's urgings to conform to high risk behaviors in order to be somebody. The kid is very likely to grab the counterfeit value and status offers that come even though there is a high price tag.

Watch initiation rituals into such naive-looking peer groups as Sub-Debutantes for middle school kids. We recently watched a sixteen-year-old grimace as she watched breakfast preparation.

"I either had to swallow a raw egg or eat a raw pig's foot at my initiation," Lila shuddered.

"Which did you choose?" I asked.

"The raw pig's foot. I couldn't look a raw egg in the face. No way! But they let me spit out the pig's foot after I chewed it. I was in."

It is clear that Lila had to prove one thing only: She would take orders of "compliance" from her senior peers. Now that she has submitted to that proof, she is an easy target to comply with any proof of womanhood they command. One Florida group allegedly has recently required that teen women must have sexual intercourse with an HIV-positive partner as proof of membership into this perpetual high-risk, life-time adolescent culture.

*Role and authority/power.* In the same way, if the kid enjoys a unique and satisfying role in the family, that enjoyment will tend to stabilize the kid even though he or she doesn't make the team or get named to Homecoming Court.

And a kid who has learned to be consistently honest, to manage money, or to be competent with laundry or other important family-taught skills tends to treasure the responsibility and authority of those character traits and skills. Such secure kids are rarely blown away by temptations to be lazy and rebellious against adults and community institutions which invite them to come on board with high participation.

So, if you shuddered in the last chapter about your competition for your kid's mind and future, look at these issues of value, status, role, and power. Also look for clues about whether your kid is comfortable and pleased about the systems to which he or she can turn, because they also can bestow role, status, value and responsibility.

## System Two: Extended Family

Your extended family consists typically of grandparents, uncles, aunts, nieces, nephews and cousins. For many kids today there are "blended" intergenerational multiple systems representing birth parents and birth kids along with step-parents and step-kids along with a birth "family of origin."

The intergenerational family—second and third degree relatives mostly—provides a system in which the growing man or woman may get informal feedback about role, status, value, responsibility and competence in a slightly larger but highly respected world of family authorities. Friendships with cousins and uncles and aunts, especially, allow the kid to see whether the "at home" family system matches the world outside. These folks live and move in other worlds, they bring other ancestries through their marrying away from your own parents' genes. There the kid who is a first or only child at home may be the end of the line of grandchildren on one side and the first and only grandchild on the other side of the house. The oldest of cousins on Dad's side of the room may find the last-of-cousins' spot in Mom's extended family. It happened to me. I was the oldest cousin in my father's clan, and the son of the youngest child, my Mother, in her clan—so the youngest cousin there.

Lance wanted to spend as much of the summer on Grandpa's farm as his parents would allow from as far back as he could remember. He liked listening to his grandparents' stories. He was always ready, even eager for everything they wanted and needed to teach him as he worked alongside both of them during the long summer days. "I got my greatest satisfaction from doing things with and for my grandparents. What was a drag to do at home for Mom and Dad," he would report as an adult, "was always a joy to do for Grandma and Grandpa." Lance's grandparents had endless interesting things that needed to be done: repairing machines and buildings, blanching, cutting and freezing sweet corn, bringing the melons to production and harvest in early fall—scores of skills Lance loved to learn and brag about when he got home. Grandpa took him to the county agent when he was thirteen to get a license to operate the farm tractor. Back in middle school, Lance flashed the license among his friends. His new "authority" linked with his real role, status, value and responsibility during the summers living with his grandparents in another state. Back at home, his parents wondered why he showed little energy for pitching in and helping around the house.

Spin these extended family systems any way you like, and celebrate your kid's many options—many ways of discovering what it is to be part of this family, to accumulate skills long valued in the family, and to learn how to be human in a particular tradition.

The risks, of course, include your child's having to deal with the family's irregular members—those who may carry compulsive addictions or who may consider it their job to "initiate" your kid into some destructive practices. But where the extended family's many systems provide variations of the home-based family values, the benefits are enormous. When grandparents live far away or are no longer available, intergenerational exposure can often be arranged by "adopting" nearby surrogate relatives whose affirmation can bless a coming generation of kids.

## System Three: Community

The family and extended family eventually become too small, too isolated from the real and large world for a kid to be assured of role, status, value, and competent responsibility for facing adult life. Enter non-related models, ministers, and other mentors whose presence in your kid's life can profoundly shape and ground adult formation!

Listen to your kid when a totally enthralled middle-schooler comes home quoting an awesome minister, teacher, or coach. Your first tendency is to be annoyed when the name surfaces a half-dozen times during one meal. The admired teacher is the obvious resident expert on everything! We endured hearing daily references to "Mr. Koos" for several months as first John and later Mike set their authority grounding on the utterances of this most admired mentor. We got acquainted with Mr. Koos, of course, and were delighted to find that he was worth imitating. We wondered where his special charisma came from, but it produced magical effects in each of our sons. Their admiration of Mr. Koos served them well as they began to see themselves as adventurers into the world of adults beyond our family circle.

Your children will locate these alternative "super model mentors" and often secretly—or openly!—wish they had been born in the home of their favorite coach, minister or other hero. They might be startled to see behind closed doors that their mentor, caught in the act of parenting a child of the same age and potential as your kid, is not as attractive when doing the parenting tasks. All of us find comfort in seeing our own parenting agendas as quite different from the mentoring opportunities that come with working with other people's kids. So parents can rejoice that there are ministers and mentors out there for their kids to choose. But the long-term identity and support come from parents.

We realized only long after the Mr. Koos years that a mentor is chosen by the "unilaterally respecting" candidate, and is chosen to perform services parents rarely perform spontaneously for their own kids. A mentor is, like the parent in early childhood years, "Larger than life! Perfect!" and worth imitating in speech, and citing as authority. This admiration of a mentor amounts to taking the measure of the man or woman, and hoping that he or she may become a carbon copy of the mentor. Every human deserves for most of their adult life to be connected to a series of mentors—these non-family admired "others." Mentors cannot easily do parent work without forfeiting the role of nurturing and blessing mentor. Parents are responsible for protecting the child, coaching the child to effective and acceptable behavior. Mentors are exclusively limited to blessing the candidate, seeing the potential, and bringing the candidate alongside where learning and more affirmation occurs along the way. When a mentor tries to correct, criticize, or financially underwrite the candidate, the mentor tends to turn into a surrogate parent and effective mentoring has ended.

These community mentors, teachers, ministers and others, along with peers in the neighborhood with whom endless hours of play established long-term friendships, form a system of people who shape your kid. And your son or daughter is very alert to evaluating how well they are regarded on those role, status, value, and responsibility issues. A system emerges here, in which the kid will know that "When I'm with these folks, I'm special. I can always 'come home' to the neighborhood."

As your child grows older and moves occasionally, there are friends left behind, important connections to school and church, special confidential comrades with whom a friendship can spring up again whenever they find themselves in touch.

## System Four: Work and Weekly Connections

For thirteen years or more your kid's "workplace" is school. Since every kid looks beyond home and relatives to discover value, status, role and responsibility readings, school is the obvious big investment time and energy bank. So discover there what life is about, what is "in" or "out" for the narrow band of a single generation—seldom more than a one- or two-year age span. You provided abundant time in the early months and years surrounding your child with the family of origin system. But when day care, kindergarten, and school opened arms to your child, the balance of time likely shifted to your kid's school "workplace."

Sheer investment of time tilts the power of influence to the schooling models—teacher and peers. So powerful is the perpetual adolescence conspiracy forged between the electronic media, music, TV and video symbols, and endorsement by teen idols that by the senior high school years, the family may watch as the child falls under the spell of seducing alien models, dangerous mentors, and values.

Most often the mentoring magnet turns toward impressive, visible, and experienced slightly older peers. This three- or four-year age group tends to form an exclusive cultural pocket, organized around idols, music, and movies, TV and video images. So powerful are the high school and university cultures, that one of my colleagues observes that any marriage of people more than four years different in age places them in a cross-cultural marriage.

Mostly that peer system consists of school-age mates and occasional adult mentors, especially those cast in extended after-hours activities. But systems experts also link up recreational organizations such as youth soccer, football, and swimming. These systems involve coaches as potential mentors associated with high training and extracurricular achievements which can powerfully attract your kid's attention and satisfaction. You will hope that there are positive, worthy near-peers in church, athletic programs, and community connections. You will pray a lot as your teens show signs of needing outside models. The ministry, youth worker volunteers at your church, and coaching staffs frequently provide magnetic mentoring resources, so you will pray, sweat, and check out your protégé's nominees. You will rightly want to verify that the magnet adult mentors are constructive for your kids in every way. In these vulnerable years the adult and peer mentors and surrogate parent types are often seen by kids as wiser and more powerful than good old Mom and Dad.

Ministers and other mentors will try to "read" the potential protégé connections. And one of the most delightful roles to play is that of broker. When you see the protégé respect or admiration at work, often you will be able to coach a teacher or other significant adult into very effective mentoring with that kid.

Todd enjoyed his family system, but at fourteen he was charmed by the skills of white-water rafting. A college professor from the community hosted a teen white-water rafting club, and Todd was energized by the new skills, the camaraderie of the group, and the mystique of the larger-than-life mentor with unusual outdoor skills—compared to a family without much time for leisure and recreation.

Trace your son's or daughter's peer system and the additional mentor potentials which surround that world of work and play in which he or she lives and moves. You will have a new respect—or terror—for the competing system to which your kid is drawn. The peer system from school or the dominant culture is one which invests role, status, value, and authority in visible and consistent ways:

*Role.* What is your kid's "job" in the weekly recreation connection or at school? How much pleasure does your kid take with that role assignment? Was it volunteered or was your kid drafted to play the role? Is your kid the hero, the clown, the egghead, the dumbo, the jock, the greaser? How does your kid fit in with that dominant, time-enveloping system? What clues do you see that playing the assigned role energizes your kid? However offended you may be at the temporary identity, this crucial role indicator tells how bonded your kid may be to those peers and the role he or she has embraced in their system.

*Status.* Is there a pecking order in your kid's school or other weekly connection system? Is your kid following orders, wearing clothes, adopting language and lifestyle coming down the chain of command beyond your doors? What dues does your child pay to get recognition? Who does your kid give orders to? Is "follower" or "leader" showing up as you glance across a week's evidence?

*Value.* What am I worth in each of my systems? Your kid will be weighing this question day and night and choosing where to attach trust and loyalty. After ten years of full time schooling, good luck. By sheer magnitude of time invested, school has taken the lion's share of your kid's attention and energy. Some of the indicators of value include a sense of being needed, being trusted with urgent tasks, hearing names or titles of empowerment, consistently being treated fairly, and being protected from abuse and harassment. Is your kid's dominant culture system enhancing a sense of self-respect? If the school experience includes shame and humiliation—from peers and perhaps from teachers and administrators—or if the home experience moves on shame and insult, the kid will tend to regard those as normal ways of treating people close to them. The kid feels like a worthless blob, so making others feel worthless seems natural. Such a kid will pick up the language of violence and putdown. These speak autobiographically, denoting the kid's emptiness and self-contempt.

*Authority.* What new skills are you seeing? These are evidences of self-initiated responsibility and effectiveness. Peers are eager to bestow status and invest authority, often requiring "delivery" of service or goods acquired through using peer-defined methods and skills. Is your kid a confidant of peers, a counselor, the "wheels," the negotiator with competing centers of conflict—a power broker? Try to imagine the sense of fulfillment that comes from carrying these kinds of trusted responsibility with peers.

## Who Will Empower Your Kid?

In this chapter I have wanted you to review the roster of candidates who are competing for the right to preside over your child's initiation into the adult world:

> Your Household
> The Kid's Extended Families
> Community Ministers and Other Mentors
> Work and Weekly Connections

Somewhere, you have spotted the folks who will likely initiate your kid into a new career—something that will match the physique and the intelligence carried between the ears. You may be wondering whether your son or daughter is fully enthralled with the prospect of becoming an alive-to-the-fingertips adult engaging all of life and responsibility with high energy and pleasure. If not, one of the competing systems has offered your kid a way to grab the keys to the fast lane without being encumbered by the boring and drab penalties of chores and work as punishment for being a kid. So take a second look at who is competing for your kid.

# 4

# What Has Gone Wrong
# With Our Culture?

I was second to get the call that Lonnie was in the Baylor Hospital emergency room. I arrived at 4:30 a.m. on Easter morning. Lonnie's mother got the first call based on his driver's license address. At nineteen, Lonnie lived at home. His father, an alcoholic, was doing his weekend thing and had not been home since he left for work on Friday morning.

Lonnie was broken up and in serious condition. His front seat partner, Mel, had few abrasions, but his neck was broken and his spinal cord seriously damaged. He would never walk again. Lonnie would walk out of the hospital in less than a week—on crutches supporting a broken leg that would mend in six weeks.

Both had "driving under the influence" levels of alcohol in their blood. And the drinking was part of a larger game of "chicken" which had them driving without lights at 2:00 a.m. in a showdown with other players. Lonnie yielded and took a tree instead of the head-on with his opponent. It was a ritual of risk and potential mixing of blood and steel, connecting testosterone to yearning for dominance, for passing the test of initiation. "Becoming a man" required some suitably challenging ceremony. His buddies defined the rules of the game.

## What Every Kid Needs

I've been working with you on a basic idea: *Every parent wants to conceive, nurture, and launch a full-grown and glorious human being. And every kid is born with a matching target—to adore these god-like adult humans and imitate their every move and mood.*

This beautiful reciprocal dream appears in every generation and arrives with deep needs which emerge on schedule. How these deep yearnings are satisfied depends on what options are available. In the early months and years, parents are the exclusive targets of the kid's unilateral respect and define the kid's internal feelings of constraint or obligation, showing in non-verbal and subtle ways what the kid thinks the parent really wants the child to be, to say, and to do. Then, during the years from ten to fifteen, the healthy kid is sure to set out in search of an adult beyond the family. The kid will turn that same adoration, respect, and imitation toward some attractive mentor to shape the launch into the kid's own adult journey. I've named the four agendas of need before, but review them here:

*Role.* When the "good life" looks like the parent's or the mentor's way of being and working, you are their fixed target, and you are delighted that a kid would want to grow up to be exactly like you. Kids like these see themselves taking up adult and parent responsibilities which match their height, weight, and sexual ripening. You can worry about young kids whose parents have crashed and burned in some tragic divorce or other disappointing failure, especially those who have not turned outward in search of a mentor. Fortunately, as a kid breaks into pubescence, the outward search for a model adult as mentor can help to cope with catastrophic losses at home.

Lance shared his story in one of my classes. His parents divorced and he and his mother were alone. In school his performance crashed. But a perceptive junior high teacher phoned his mother and asked to take mother and son to dinner at a restaurant. There the family disruption was drawn on the table. The teacher urged Lance to go out for basketball. He was the coach as well as Lance's math teacher, and the season was just ready to begin. Lance's mother commented that there was no way to do that, since she worked and could not pick Lance up after late practice every day. The teacher offered to be the transportation. The rest of the story is poetry. Today Lance is graduating and moving into his calling as a pastor.

But "role" experiments are most often rooted in "job" assignments received in the early years. In Lance's case, the teacher simply threw the door open for Lance to see the role as being a competent adult and doing interventions in behalf of others in need. Some roles are chosen in early childhood as the kid searches for some unique place in the family.

My friend Don Bowen reports that his earliest memories are of a mother who was in the final stages of heart disease. With older siblings in the family,

Don remembers wondering what he could do to help Mother be happy and maybe live a little longer. He decided that he would make it his job to keep her laughing.

Today, decades after losing his mother—who managed to survive to see him grown—Don Bowen is in high demand as a speaker, emcee, and comedian. In the circle of friends where we often move, we cannot carry on a serious conversation for more than a few minutes before Don breaks in with some off-the-wall original piece of humor. Only after several years of enjoying him did it occur to me to ask him where this amazing gift got started.

Role more often is based on the child's adoration of the parents' or the mentor's job or skill. But a crisis in the family can turn a kid toward some chosen compensatory role. The role of clown or comedian is often picked up as the positive way to cope with some family crisis or trauma. The "hero" is the rescuing kid who gets the highest rewards from coming through for the family's honor. But surrogate husband or surrogate wife are also roles sometimes assumed by children who accept the challenge of being there for an abandoned parent, taking the typical gender role responsibility of a missing or a disabled parent. All of these are adult roles rehearsed by children and rewarded in the family. These stories illustrate how a kid uniquely defines the personal role and takes it. And they may also suggest how important it is for kids to have healthy alternatives available when they need to fix their aspirations for a lifetime.

Look at a diagram of the child in search of adult role, status, and value. Here is what the kid deserves, and the family is the first and most empowering agency to deliver on those basic needs:

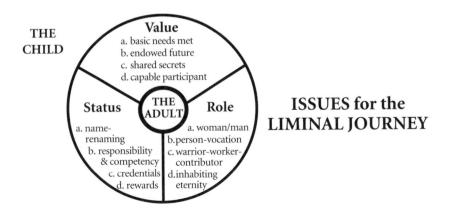

*Status.* When the environment is vital and stable, every kid wants to grow up to take adult responsibility. Every kid looks into the mirror, compares height and weight with the biggest folks in the house. You have been there to see how much an emerging teenager enjoys looking down on the shortest adult in the clan. Often a shrinking grandparent is the happy target for the kid's claim of superiority of height. Families which celebrate physical maturing, keeping track of height by dates written on the doorjam in the laundry room are cultivating hope and offering a promise that appropriate privileges and responsibilities are just above the next notch in the yardstick. Growing up in such an environment is a promise of a ticket into the adult world.

But if nobody seems to notice, or if family members are in open warfare over the menacing threat of a kid grown tall and strong, with sexual powers to bring humiliation or arrest or disease to the household, the kid will likely turn elsewhere. There are other markets which appreciate the new body, the new energy, and the potential money and flesh that can be exploited. Those hucksters of hype are eager to seduce the kid into believing that the initiation and its required lifestyle are gifts of pleasure and crowning gifts of true gang or peer status earned. The exploitive plastic mentors of TV, stage, screen, and video have no conscience and are ready to seduce your kid. The gang, the drug dealer, and the skin and flesh dealers lure away our emerging pubescent kids in droves. With all kids, it is crucial that the teacher, coach, minister or other mentor be a person of highest integrity. When a kid becomes a protégé of a chosen mentor who is still a confused adolescent, or who is irresponsible with money, truth, or sex, the protégé stands to become a victim at the hands of a person who was fully trusted.

*Value.* The easy transition comes when the child is aware of having authentic value to the parents, ministers and mentors. You forge an early partnership with the kid. You share work and coach in skill development at every common, household, community, and gender-specialty task. You create celebrations to mark completion of major tasks. Such kids are virtually unshakable by seductive ploys from the peer culture and the electronic media.

Blessed is the kid whose parent never assigns drudgery work as solitary punishment to be done alone, but instead conspires, "Let's hit that yard work (or laundry, or home repair, or remodeling, or sewing, or putting the mailing out for the family business) tonight. Can you handle your homework before seven o'clock? Then when we've licked the job, we'll celebrate at your favorite recreation or restaurant."

If, however, the kid picks up clues of being a financial liability, a social inconvenience, or a clumsy and bothersome kid who is incompetent to share any of the adult's trust and tasks, the potential sense of value evaporates. For such a kid, self-value or self-respect may never fill the cup of energy and vitality to make the journey to adult competency and productivity. For those who partner with parents and mentors, they tend to be so energized with adult productivity that they will regard work as recreation for a lifetime. Symptoms of low self-respect range from angry rebellion and arrogance—a facade to hide the emptiness—to sullenness or other depression behavior. Occasionally the kid exercises the terminal choice of self-rejection: suicide. If family messages seem to suggest or outright declare, "We wish you had never been born," the kid may well reason that it is never too late to abort a child. By the teen years a kid can exercise the "choice." Robert Coles, in his *Moral Intelligence of Children*,[1] suggests that even before a child is born, the mother's and father's attitude toward the pregnancy will plant positive mental attitudes toward life and values or toxic ones. Ministers and other mentors frequently rescue a kid with predispositions of self-rejection, but often are baffled to understand where such dark and dangerous ideas of worthlessness have come from.

*Responsibility and Authority.* When a young child learns how to operate a vacuum cleaner or a dust rag, the stage is set for empowering the kid as colleague, helper, and a solver of emergency problems when a crisis occurs which requires quick execution of such a task. "Grandma called. She's coming over, but this house looks terrible. Can you help me put it in shape? She's on the way now." And the young child's "authority" turns into an essential and happy "power move" as the job is done quickly and the family's honor is polished in the eyes of a welcome visitor. Competency and responsibility become a positive addiction when kids experience the power of productive work.

Small chunks of responsibility and authority are handed over piece by piece as the child is recruited, trusted, and brought on the production team for a thousand happy tasks. But the big chunks of power and authority easily turn into rituals of initiation, celebrations of marker points in development and achievement. Car keys and a gift certificate for driving lessons all delivered on the sixteenth birthday constitute a major rite of passage.

"But I don't even know how to drive," Melissa queried her parents as she lifted the ring with keys to the family automobile from the gift box.

---

[1]Robert Coles, *Moral Intelligence of Children*. New York: Random House, 1997.

"I know," Melissa's dad said, "but we look forward to the day you get your license. You can get your permit now, and we know you are ready to help with the complicated transportation schedule here."

But look what happens when no significant adults will initiate the kids into adulthood. They will leap to initiate each other:

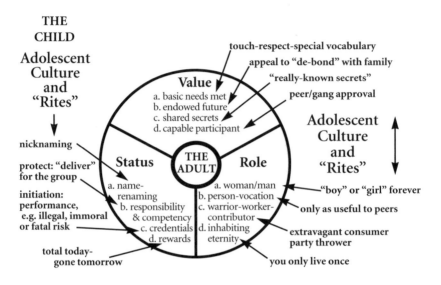

## ISSUES FOR THE LIMINAL JOURNEY

If the kid is held hostage, however, and if no markers loom on the far horizon to welcome the kid into significant adult role, status, value, and authority, then behold: the dark competition occurs. Enter the siren songs of the electronic media and the desperate peer culture:

> *Come along with us!*
> *Let us give you the secret test!*
> *Leap at our every command!*
> *We will take you into the fast lane.*
> *Show off your stuff! Then we'll show you the money!*
> *Give us your potential, then you get our endorsement.*
> *Sure, we cannot deliver you into authentic adulthood,*
> *But who wants to be a boring Man or Woman anyway?*
> *"Boy" or "Girl" is your forever destiny.*
> *Walk through our rituals of risk and blood and secret mysteries.*

*Membership is certified in your blood, your scars, and your viruses!*
*Be one of us. Membership marks you as cool, laid back, indifferent!*
*Take your entitlement to lifetime of non-producing, high-consuming*
*  adolescence.*
*Only a fool would trade this gig for embracing growing up.*

## What Has Gone Wrong?

Social commentators everywhere are trying to figure out why kids' SAT scores are going down. They speculate why teenage pregnancy is rising, why juvenile crime is skyrocketing, and why teen suicides are soaring. Any reflective person of any age can easily ask any number of questions beginning with "Why?"

David Barton, lecturer and video producer, with his *America's Godly Heritage* and its spinoff called *Salute to America*[2] appearing at military installations across the country, makes a convincing argument about what has gone wrong. He documents how the present descent into chaos was triggered when, in 1953, the Supreme Court ruled against prayer in public schools, abandoning the standard practice of writing the case to demonstrate how the current ruling is grounded in historic precedent. Then, in the same rootless way a few years later, the Supreme Court legitimized abortion. These landmark decisions were written from a "blank slate," deliberately abandoning the entire history of legal precedent and values in the U.S. The Court's bold break from history into existential relativism throws light on the now widely visible exaltation of fashionable political correctness, which violates fixed moral grounding, and helps us to understand how Americans elect to public office persons of moral ambivalence. From the dates of those relativistic Supreme Court decisions, our rising flood of adolescent problems and tragedies threaten to undo our culture and perhaps end Western civilization.

H. Stephen Glenn, in an amazing video, *Developing Capable Young People*, and in his parallel book, *Raising Self-Reliant Children in a Self-Indulgent World*,[3] cites World War II as the national crisis which put fathers into military service and mothers into the workplace. Houses abandoned by adults turned children into latchkey kids. Glenn, in a speech to national educational leaders, now put on video, points out how these children of affluence now tend to use

---

[2]See David Barton, *America's Godly Heritage*. Aledo, TX: Wall Builders, Inc., PO Box 397. Phone 817-441-6044, 1992. See also Barton, *Education and the Founding Fathers*, 1991.

[3]H. Stephen Glenn, *Raising Self-Reliant Children in a Self-Indulgent World*. New York: St. Martin's Press, 1989. Video: *Developing Capable Young People*. Box 318, Lexington, SC 29072.

guilt to keep parents working in order to pay for socially acceptable brandname clothes and vehicles. He documents how these post-World War II teens were the turning point population on which SAT scores began to drop off the charts. The decline in SAT scores is mirrored by the rise in every negative teen culture trend including crime, teen pregnancy, and suicide.

Urie Bronfenbrenner, who hosted Forum 15 of the 1970 White House Conference on Children, may have been the first to see danger coming. He observed in "Report of Forum 15" that we are part of a culture in which a broken television set gets more attention and arouses more energy than a broken child. We have, he said, lost the art of turning children into humans, and all of us are losers because of the family rat race.

## Families That Win

In spite of all of these tragic patterns of failure, families in the sixties, seventies, eighties and nineties still have had internal resources to stabilize their children and launch them well. Families who kept priorities on abiding values, and survived the onslaught of urgent political and social pressure, found strategies that worked. Here are key issues which never change:

*Time.* Every family is running at top speed simply to meet daily schedules for everybody. Today, most two-parent households seem to need two adult incomes to support the family's lifestyle, mortgages, and payments on multiple vehicles. The home has often become a sort of human traffic intersection. Parent-child interaction dips as low as 37 seconds per day, almost exclusively devoted to urgent words of advice, correction, and problem solving.

Since World War II everybody's choices about activities and material goods have skyrocketed in complexity. No one today can recognize and name every automobile by make and model when they scan traffic on the highway. Before World War II it was simple, easy to do. The most exotic marketplace in the world used to be the Sears & Roebuck or Montgomery Ward mail-order catalogues. No more. They are gone, and in their places are Wal-Mart, Kmart, Sam's Place, Best Buy, and Circuit City—all eager to provide gratification for our many desires.

And we are pulled toward church, school, clubs, Little League, community recreation's football and soccer, plus the full array of contact and private competition sports through the schools. We must by all means enroll our kids and see them through private music, art, and ballet. Beyond this there are demands for parents' time as volunteers at church, school, and in all of the above as drivers, coaches, sponsors, and parent club officers.

Without significant time at meals, in the car, and during the hour ahead of bedtime, a child cannot possibly feel attached to parents. A thoughtful child has no reason to respect and long for a place in the adult world which has depleted their parents' energy, turning them into mechanical problem solvers when emergencies strike.

So all of us are forced to the unpleasant question: How do you decide among the plethora of entrées which time demands are top priorities and deserve full family attention? Could the family face the options and choose together? Where do relationships rank? Are the people, like throwaway products, merely dispensable? Where will we find time to turn a child into a human being?

*Celebration.* Without time, there is scarcely a way to celebrate the many victories or to grieve the losses which occur repeatedly in our overcrowded weeks of rat racing. But families can put themselves on the schedule, block out time to be there for each other, to be at home instead of away. In these reserved blocks of time, families can celebrate a birthday, a report card, or a new and special friendship. But what if there is no "natural high" of emotion and endorphins, triggered by sensations of well-being and closeness? If not, our children will be vulnerable to the "artificial highs" of high-risk. They are vulnerable to indulge in secret or flagrant misadventures which trigger the adrenaline high of compulsive appetite or dip into the temporary "fix" of the fast lane of hype and drugs. Everybody needs sensations of warmth and closeness. But toxic and often deadly highs provided by peers and strangers are better than nothing—or at least they feel better than the loneliness of a new kind of cold brought on by the frosty winter of an empty house and the typical 37 seconds of high-voltage parent reactions every day.[4]

*Trust.* Every young kid believes that you can tell the truth at home, show any hurting body part to parents at home, that parents are first-aid and fix-it professionals. Before the doctor sees the injured body, Mother and Daddy will check it out. So also with secrets: when a boundary is violated, parents need to know, because today's emotional or sexual abuse is like the child's injuries yesterday. If it was a bad day at school, when the door opens at home, a

---

[4]See Urie Bronfenbrenner, "Report of Forum 15—Children and Parents: Together in the World," in *Report to the President: White House Conferences on Children* (Washington, D. C.: Government Printing Office, 1970). For further treatment see Bronfenbrenner's *The Two Worlds of Childhood: USA and USSR.* (New York: Simon and Schuster, 1972) especially the chapter "The Unmaking of the American Child."

trusting kid can burst into tears and be comforted—unless, of course, you are home alone for a couple of hours. Then where do you turn?

And if things are shaky at home, you can phone or run to a minister or other mentor. So these teachers, coaches, and volunteers in community services to the young occasionally find that a crisis has driven a kid to seek help outside the family. We have taken in a half-dozen teens across the decades until things at home stabilized and it was safe to go home again.

Kids turn to whoever is there. So you pray that there are competent and safe ministers and other mentors available. Sometimes the child has nowhere to turn. They have to swallow their pain, button up their wounds. They can't expose the humiliation at school because it might bring more humiliation on the street outside their front door. Sometimes the after-school adventures on the street are laced with high risk—the triple-X-rated videos a neighbor kid shares with yours, for example.[5] The neighbor kid has found the videos stashed behind the movie videos in the family room. Our children sometimes carry community secrets. They worry that adults and families would explode if the obscenities were discovered. Trust shifts from the family to peers as children conspire to cover up a community moral crisis. When parents, ministers or other mentors finally discover the chaos, then intervention is sometimes more difficult and options are fewer. We grieve that this conspired peer evil sometimes makes it tough for a kid we love to enter the adult domain as an honest and constructive member of the community, given their perception that there were no adults they could trust in their time of trouble.

So, what can a kid really believe? Who is there? Why is there no live flesh-and-blood adult at home when the child's day is ending? Is the adult way of life really something to long for if it is only a career in which parents spend 37 seconds per day of negative coaching with their children? Is that all there is to adulthood? Is that really "parenting"? And children? Why would anybody have kids if they couldn't make time for them and celebrate regularly as a family?

---

[5] I often think of the 15-year-old young man at a conference in Estes Park, Colorado, who tearfully described his sexual initiation at 13 when a neighbor girl lured him to watch her father's hidden XXX-rated videos. The two of them eventually experimented with duplicating with their own bodies what they were seeing on the screen. He was responding to my invitation to "do the work of mourning" which Jesus blessed in "Blessed are those who mourn." I had suggested that whenever there are past experiences we now wished we had never had, grief was the appropriate homework assignment.

In this chapter I've wanted you to see that today's teen contemplates bleak and painful prospects in our deteriorating culture. Can you hear the fatalistic internal exploration? Resolved: I will be forever a teenager and grow old without buying into this way of pretending to fall in love, marry, and have children. It is no life at all to go through the motions of adulthood if it is such a boring life. I'll extend childhood. I'll stick with this modern invention called adolescence and see whether I can stay on this merry-go-round for a lifetime.

Fortunately, these distortions about "adulthood" are not all there is. And we are ready now to turn to the options open to parents, ministers and other mentors as they bring our young to the launching pad of productive and fulfilling adult lives.

# 5

# Who Invented Adolescence?

I met Gary during a low point in his seven-year effort at finishing college. He was funded by parents who were baffled at his college pattern. He consistently registered for a full load of academic hours, then would drop them after the deadline for a refund. He was lucky to complete a couple of classes with a credit of D or better each semester. His professional-level parents were ready to fund not only his college expenses at a private school, but to furnish emergency bailout money as well.

Gary was depressed, suicidal he said, when he phoned. Could he come in and talk? He had date-raped Betty, a talented college woman, and wanted to marry her. He couldn't live without her. Yes, he had been having sex more or less all the time since he was fifteen. No, he didn't expect to graduate, ever. This was a good place to put in several years at his parents' expense. Yes, he could always go home and live with his family. They never hassled him about anything, he told me.

Marijuana and occasional parties with cocaine and LSD enveloped Gary's depression and bothered him with flashbacks of peripheral light streaks that distorted everything in his vision.

That was fifteen years ago. Gary is now thirty-nine. Betty, his date-rape victim, responded to his pitiful con game, came back, and married him. She has worked without relief, paid his bills and furnished housing for nearly a dozen years. He has worked occasionally. His jobs, mostly contract odd-jobs of painting, put money into his drinking and secret life away from home. Betty has finally sent him on his way. Since he is out of the house, he has found an equally unemployed and listless friend who has space where he can camp out for now.

## What Is Wrong with This Picture?

Before World War II in North America, boys turned into men and girls into women in a pretty tight ritual that included a driver's license at 16, high school graduation at 18, and love, marriage, sex, and pregnancy by age 20, plus or minus two years! Kids were out of the house, if only down the road or up the street. They had plenty of encouragement and support, and families served as underwriters for their larger risks, should a calamity strike the young household.

Gary's story, now commonplace, was only true for one in a thousand forty years ago, and they were regarded as anomalies. Such unmotivated young adults were regarded as the black sheep, the delinquents. Whole communities wrung their hands at the thought that such a boy was a lost soul who probably wouldn't ever be able to get life together and make it work right.

Today, many young men and women are unable to stick with anything. Of course their live-ins are temporary. So are their marriages, almost inevitably. As Paul Pearsall has reminded us in his 1988 best seller, *Super-Marital Sex: Loving for Life,*[1] "Sex is not like tennis. Practice does not make perfect. It only leads to more practice." So when these morally and emotionally disabled perpetual adolescents walk out on their own young children, they have grown accustomed to going home again. They are "guests" in their childhood homes and are addicted to an extravagant "guest status" lifestyle.

In contrast, they are so disoriented to life that they regard normal adult investments of energy as a waste. They cannot imagine plugging in to the boring world of career, marital fidelity, and parenting. So they opt for the perpetual adolescent life of high spending and single extravagance. When that collapses, they try to come home again, expecting to turn once more to their customary addictions to hyperactivity, adrenaline rushes and teen-like diversions. They live for the weekends which, after all, are touted as "made for Michelob," as are one-night stands, pickups at the singles bar, or cruises through the gay strip of the city.

---

[1]Paul Pearsall, *Super-Marital Sex: Loving for Life.* New York: Doubleday, 1987.

## Adolescence: Crazy-Making Our Kids

We invented adolescence. We decided that kids were a liability, that they were a luxury.

We had children, like we bought cars and furniture, to sort of be in style. There weren't any household or farm tasks in which a kid would prove useful, so when they came into our homes, we tried to entertain them. And parents have been matched in kind by most ministers and youth volunteers. Even teachers and coaches feed the adolescent appetites. Churches tend to program to the fast lane, with extravagant and expensive trips which indulge the adolescent entertainment and fat-living expectations which permeate our culture. Too often a high school coach feeds the "sex for scoring" appetites of teens, while professional stars on court or field brag about their sexual adventures with fans. Even parents may find themselves confused or fascinated by the new ethic and vicariously relive their own emerging adult powers, wishing they had had an opportunity for extravagance, experimentation, and promiscuity. When this parental fascination occurs, they are likely to feed the indulgent and destructive potentials of their children, funding their beer busts, city sprees, and beach house weekends. Such parents often tend to indulge in an affair or two in light imitation of the carefree "adolescence" they cut short. And roughly half of them will divorce in order to experiment with another live-in or marriage.

## An American Invention

The American invention of adolescence occurred when sexual ripening dropped from an average age of eighteen for girls in 1840, down to twelve for girls in 1990. For boys the shift was from age nineteen on average, down to thirteen. Across the same span of our history, we postponed admitting our kids into the adult world of competent adult work and marriage. The legal age for marriage moved from pubescence in pre-industrial America, to eighteen for women and twenty-one for men in most states. In most states today, "Equal Rights" has declared eighteen the age of majority for both men and women. With the invention of adolescence and the unending educational agenda of modern times, everyone agrees that our young cannot afford to marry and become parents. Behold! We turn to science for birth control and to the Supreme Court for a blessing on abortion. We unleash sexually explicit entertainment accompanied by electronic heroes who demonstrate the "new extravagant consumption and sex norms" and feed our young compelling advertising for extravagant consumption and safe but promiscuous sex. It is no surprise that we miss the "gate of adulthood" as the age of first marriage for males has skyrocketed from nineteen to twenty-six since World War II. So our kids are "all dressed up with no place to go" for more than ten years. And we have created a free zone of irresponsibility called "adolescence" that has introduced the loss of adult identity, fidelity in exclusive marriage, and the joys of being parents.

Remember that *adolescence refers to the time gap between sexual ripening (average age of twelve for girls and thirteen for boys) and the privileges of adult work and marriage (average age of twenty-five+ for males' first marriage today).* Post-World War II males married at twenty (98 percent were married before age twenty-five), and had hit pubescence on an average at age fifteen, with a clear target of being an adult with career, wife, and kids. The ten-year pressure cooker was devoted to pursuing the marriage and calculating the plan for establishing another home and family.

You can read more about the "invention of adolescence" in my *Risk-Proofing Your Family.*[2] Professor Ron Koteskey, taking early cues from me, has written extensively on this secular trend of earlier ripening of adults.[3] You can also see charts showing the declining age of sexual ripening in any developmental psychology or physiological psychology book. You will also see occasional references to this secular trend of early physical maturing in the popular magazines and newspapers. It seems to be associated with increasing artificial light in cultural environments, with earlier significant mixing of the sexes, and with diet, especially from meat derived from animals fed with hormonally-boosted, fast-growth mixtures of grains and chemicals.

## Instant Adults—Straight from Child to Maturity

Before World War II, every teen longed to embrace full adulthood. Children's games were efforts at doing what adults do. Toy stores prospered because they offered miniature household and garden and farm tools and

---

[2]See my *Risk-Proofing Your Family.* Pasadena: The U. S. Center for World Mission's William Carey Publishing Division, 1995. Chapters 1-7 are the foundation for this book. I go into detail there on defining adolescence, the "secular trend" with its earlier physiological development. There and in my *Bonding: Relationships in the Image of God* are documented various theories about what drives the earlier pubescence across the generations—the "secular trend," the continuing lowering of the age of biological ripening. See chapter 8 in *Bonding.* Its title is: "Launching Your Teens: Is There Life After Puberty?"

[3]Ronald L. Koteskey, *Understanding Adolescence.* Victor, 1987. His summary of the same theoretical base is more recently in "Adolescence as a Cultural Invention," in Donald Ratcliff and James Davies, *Handbook of Youth Ministry.* Birmingham: Religious Education Press, 1991.

gadgets with which children could pretend to be doing what they wanted to grow up to do: work as their parents worked.

But when children were no longer an asset to assist with family business or farm production, they became twenty-year guests to be entertained and launched into the good life of extravagant consumption. The kids bought the shift in curriculum. They were glad to compete with neighbor kids in their accumulation of extravagant toys and clothing. Today children play with electronic toys and virtually none of it rehearses or simulates productive adult career activity. But look at what we took away from the kids.

Three things have to happen for girls to become women and for boys to become men:

1. They have to become competent, productive human beings;
2. They need to be empowered to search for a life identity and mission and for a partner who shares a vision that matches theirs;
3. They need to ripen healthily and become sexually capable of entering into an intimate and child-producing marriage.

These are the classical prerequisites in every culture when we look at the timing for conducting rites of passage as children become adults.

America today is the scene of a great media and business community conspiracy to make adolescence a permanent lifestyle. The entertainment industry promotes the fad and style corporations which fund the entertainment industry in a gigantic marketing-money feeding frenzy. These greedy corporations are preying on the wallets of the nation's parents, whose leisured teens shame and haggle them into greater and greater chunks of the family's cash flow. These teens deck themselves in brand names and speak authoritatively on the latest music, videos, and obscene movies.

No doubt our culture invented adolescence slowly and almost accidentally. Watch what happened:

1. Our young ripened physically at younger ages and were physically ready for adult responsibility ahead of their grandparents. But,
2. We elevated their schooling requirements and employment prerequisites higher and higher.
3. We abolished apprenticeships and cooperative education opportunities in the workplace.

4. We toughened labor regulations, indenturing young adults to minimum wage jobs which could not support an independent adult, much less an adult with spouse and children. Suddenly,

5. After their dues were paid in schooling and internships, they found themselves being interviewed by CEOs with half the training they possessed. All the while,

6. The entertainment, music, and pornography industries combined to seduce these frustrated, isolated, out-of-the-loop-to-adulthood kids and mark them for life with shame-driven appetites and emotionally damaged souls.

## Tribal Cultures: Blood Rites of Passage

Those of us who grew up in North America or Western Europe before World War II cannot help being alarmed when we see the waste of emerging adults from fifteen to twenty-five. We may be addicted to our culture's way of amusing our youth to death. But if we are, we must face the losses incurred when poor little rich kids lose their way, die by violence at astronomical rates, and blow the top off auto insurance rates by their irresponsible use of vehicles. These are grim reminders that the American way of adolescence is not working well for anyone—we are all losers. (Before you panic with despair, jump ahead and behold the title for chapter 6: Upstaging Adolescence: How Everybody Wins!)

In stark contrast to the American failure is the much older pattern in tribal cultures in which a girl becomes a woman and a boy becomes a man in a single and often swift ceremony—a rite of passage. I want you to walk through this gallery of examples in preparation for creating effective rites of passage for our irreplaceable kids! Notice that most are blood rituals and involve reproductive potential. Notice too that our culture is damaged by blood rituals involving "losing virginity" and creating and birthing a baby.

Boys growing up among the Nuer in South Africa choose the time to experience the one-day ceremony by which they become men.

"I am ready for Gar," a boy will typically whisper to an aunt.

The aunt then pulls a two-finger "pinch" sample of hair from his scalp, examines it closely and announces with disgust, "Baby hair!"

This is the signal the young man needs to set the manhood ritual in motion. Typically he then turns to an older sister and asks her to remove his "baby hair."

She does it with a hand-held steel blade razor, until his head is cleanly shaved. A place for the surgery is in the septic yard. The ground is prepared; he rests his head on a heap of ash from the dung of the sacred cattle. A neighboring "surgeon" performs the cutting ritual—never a family member or a local resident.

The Nuer young man, lying naked, face up on the ground, never flinches while the guest initiator slices deep and bloody full circle rings entirely around his head. A half dozen of these bleeding halos circle his skull a half-inch apart. The circles will be visible as horizontal scars forever after on his forehead, but they extend around the entire head through his temple hair and around the back, to meet the starting point of the incision in the front.

The young man, bloodied by the ritual, facing upward, lifts himself on hands and feet. Naked, with belly to the sky, he slowly walks his horizontal body into a hut to recover for a couple of hours while the visiting priest sacrifices a goat, denoting the end of the young man's old life as a child and ushering in his new adult status. The community throws a celebration meal to honor the boy-turned-man. The celebrative meal revives the boy-turned-man and welcomes him into the community as an adult, with all the rights and privileges extended to all adult males.[4]

David Cohen has given us *The Circle of Life*, mostly devoted to stunning photographs of the human life cycle. His pictures and sketchy narrative devote a major treatment to rites of passage. Sample a few of the rituals Cohen pictures:

Among American Apache Indians, rituals for girls and boys are equally brief and bring a distinct entry of adult privilege.

Kota boys in the African Congo are painted blue for several days, signifying the ghost-like disappearance of their childhood. During the ritual days they are "invisible" to adults. Once the ritual occurred at age nine. But today it is postponed until the mid-teens when schooling is finished. Even so, the blue mask days provide a clear marker point at which they enter the adult world and are taken seriously by the community.

A girl at onset of menarche in Cairo, Egypt, is forcibly restrained while her Muslim father circumcises her by removing her clitoris. This practice, illegal in most countries, persists in many. Estimates of the number of Muslim and

---

[4]Robert Gardner and Hilary Harris, video recording, *The Nuer*. Del Mar, Calif., CRM/McGraw-Hill Films, 1970.

Coptic girls who are initiated by this family clitoridectomy run as high as seventy-five percent.

Cohen pictures a newly pubescent boy in an Italian family ritual. He is being passed, naked, through the split trunk of a sapling tree. Mounted within the split trunk is a small painting of the Virgin Mary. The young man's genitals pass before her painting in the liturgy which turns him from boy to man. Later the sapling is bound together to continue its growth, forever holding the secret of the manhood "passage" as the tree rises to become his towering witness in the forest.[5]

Mike Maxey, my former student and continuing colleague, who grew up among the Dani of Irian Jaya, New Guinea, brings me photos, audiotapes, and stories of the Dani. There he was honored to be invited to the boy-to-manhood ritual in which phallic sticks—"gourds," they call them—are installed to denote his manly status in the community. This singular "garment" is their first, having grown up naked. Dani girls wear a virginal grass skirt from infancy, but exchange its visual protection when they marry in a ceremony. Mike tells me the word for marriage among the Dani means the "winding on of the skirt." Naked from the waist up, her budding breasts mark her availability and the urgency of her marriage. The wedding skirt is woven of tree roots, resembling the texture of a tennis net. The skirt is literally and permanently sewn on the woman and will never be removed. She is tightly encased from waist to knees, forcing her to hobble when walking.

In Turkey, elaborate rituals of circumcision for boys of ten or so see them dressed in white silk costumes. The surgery is performed in a religious ceremony involving family members. After the circumcision, the young man is placed on an ornate bed, also decorated for the honoring ceremony. There he may be seen in Cohen's pictures, sitting on the bed, fighting back tears of pain, but facing guests who bring gifts and congratulations on his bloody arrival at manhood.

In Gabon, Eshira girls on the occasion of the first menstrual period are painted white. They are exiled into a white hut, eat only white foods, and are restricted for one year in the Mabandji rite which guarantees a diet thought to insure their good health.

In Zaire, a girl with delicately painted marks on her face enters into a Lesse ritual. She will remain isolated for one month along with other girls passing into womanhood.

---

[5]David Cohen, ed., *The Circle of Life: Rituals from the Human Family Album.* New York: HarperCollins, 1991.

Cohen's pictures include one of a Kau woman in the African Sudan. Her abdomen is rippled with patterned scars. She has been cicatrized with scarification welts which mark her transitions into menarche, into marriage, then into first childbirth. All of the markings have unique significance and together they chronicle her journey into significance as a woman.

## Blood-letting the American Way

Joseph Campbell and others of us have pointed out for more than a generation now that every child deserves a ritual consistent with the culture of origin by which passage is marked from childhood to adulthood. And we warn, repeatedly, that if parents and communities do not provide liturgies of "promotion," the kids will invent bloody rituals by which to initiate each other.

Today's American teenage initiations are traditionally defined by peers and are complete with blood price rituals. Typically they are initiated into perpetual adolescence and craziness

by counting their sexual partners,
by impregnating or being impregnated resulting in a live birth,
by accomplishing feats of extravagant speed in an automobile,
by consumption of hard liquor within a limited number of minutes, or
by bringing off criminal acts without detection.

The list of blood-risk demands is endless. Why would such vandals be rewarded by being hosted on nationally televised talk shows? The notorious Spur Posse swaggered on and off a dozen talk shows, rolled up in guest limousines, and became heroes of the electronic media and worlds of style and hype. Back home in their Los Angeles suburb, the teen women victims who were used by the Spur Posse in the accumulation of sexual penetration records were appealing for opportunities to meet them in court on charges of rape.

Then, in the fall of 1993, an American movie[6] featured a ritual initiation scene as young men lay face up on the double line of a highway in the hours past midnight. The movie triggered mimic tragedies as young men across America tried the high-risk dare as a test to prove manhood.

---

[6] I refer to the 1992 movie, *The Program*, which featured a football team. Among the high-risk adventures was a "ritual process" lying down on the double line in a dangerous section of a highway. The movie triggered copycat rituals across the U.S., with several teen deaths reported within a week of the film's opening. Produced by Touchstone Pictures; Cella Costa, Production Manager.

Now, as the century ends we have witnessed mere children using automatic weapons to slaughter unarmed schoolmates and teachers. These children and teens even maintain websites on which they post hit lists of potential targets of their planned murders. The extravagant spoiling of American children has given us a generation which lives in terror and fear of one another.

The American corruption of youth is now an epidemic wherever "imitating American" becomes the youth generation's dream. In Macedonia, the southern country formed from the former Yugoslavia, I recently inquired where the teens had learned English—perhaps in the schools?

"No. French in schools," they explained, then glowed, "We learn English from TV." In most emerging countries where electricity is working its magic, "imitating America" means:

1. Watching old American TV reruns and copying our way of "inventing adolescence" with its lifestyles of extravagant consumption. Or in more advanced countries, American programming and movies are standard elite diet with their destructive teen culture idols and rituals of admission into career adolescence.

2. Buying American fad products and flaunting the American look in clothing, consuming status beverages and narcotics, and exaggerating American teen behavior, especially flaunting alcohol consumption, drugs, marijuana, and sexual promiscuity.

3. Paralyzing the local youth culture, making it "forever adolescent" as a lifestyle for a non-productive, consumer-extravagant, playful ride into the sunset of life—without marriage, without family, without career except self-gratification at the public's expense (or on America's credit if US foreign aid will foot the bill for their continuing non-productive and indulgent lifestyles).

Cohen includes in *The Circle of Life* photo gallery pictures of young men in Rio de Janeiro, Brazil. They are self-initiating at risk of death. Teen "*surfistas*" play out a deadly and bloody scenario to prove their manhood. They go "wind surfing" riding on top of high-speed electric trains. Once their first communion in Roman Catholic tradition was an occasion for feasting and celebrating. Today they regard the ceremony as inadequate to verify their manhood. So they disappear after the First Communion and the celebrative meal, then accept the peer challenge: put on women's clothing and climb on top of the high-speed railway commuter trains. They mount the tops of the railroad cars which are electrically operated at speeds above 100 miles per hour. The young men squat, stoop, and body surf, leaning into the wind. They are wind surfing among electric service lines and the deadly obstructions above the speeding cars. In a recent year nearly two thousand Brazilian youths died by decapitation or electrocution while doing the *surfista* peer initiation ritual.

But in Ensenada, Mexico, on the Baja Peninsula, we looked for an *Iglesia Methodista Libre* one Sunday morning. We were astonished to find a large and vital congregation whose worship service was being devoted to a holy celebration of one young woman's *quincinera*, her passage into womanhood on her fifteenth birthday. The young woman, dressed in white with white lace head covering, looking much like an American bride, responded to the pastor's announcement and invitation. She came forward and took her place in a regal-looking chair in the center aisle, where the entire service of worship was presented specifically for her honor. The sermon was visibly preached directly to her, with hundreds of us as witnesses to this ritual of initiation and respect.

When the Sunday morning benediction was complete, we noticed that dozens of people, as if on cue, began further celebration. A buffet banquet was spread in the courtyard. Flash cameras suddenly appeared and the honored young woman was the visible center of a photo session, much as a bride is at her wedding.

This evangelical congregation has "taken back" a Mexican rite of passage which, in both the secular and in the traditional Mexican Roman Catholic tradition, has been portrayed as a very sensuous occasion to introduce the young woman to "adult status." It is commonly characterized by revelry, drunkenness, and sexual pressures, which culminate quickly in marriage. Cohen pictures Brazilian girls in this traditional ceremony who are saying farewell to childhood at age fifteen in elaborate *Festa de Quince Anos*.

In this chapter I have wanted you to see how the invention of adolescence in our culture is crippling most of our young before they embrace the third decade of life. I have wanted you to see that rites of passage are a special challenge, and always have been, for every tradition and culture. With these background pictures in place, we can now turn to looking at alternatives open to us for truly launching our kids effectively.

*Empower Your Kids* is an invitation to abolish the culturally-invented adolescence which is disabling our young and preventing them from seizing their productive adult vocations. The book is a gift to parents, offering alternative ways of launching and empowering healthy and productive adults who will bless themselves and their world. The book is also a manual especially designed to bring ministers, teachers, coaches, and other mentors into the scene to serve as midwives or high priests of initiation as families break with the wider culture to *empower their kids.* If we have invented adolescence, surely there is a way to re-invent dignity, empowerment, and blessing from the adult members of the family and the community. Together, we can welcome our young in rituals which far surpass their peer initiation rituals and the likely booty they will deliver—a lifetime of paralyzed dysfunction as they find themselves addicted to living in perpetual adolescence.

# 6

# Upstaging Adolescence: How Everybody Wins!

Here are three stories drawn from families who discovered that "crazy-making" in the culture was stealing their kids and seducing them into the peer subculture with its toxic patterns.

Walk through an awakening with Roy and Charlene. They went to bed with a deep worry they couldn't quickly resolve. "Are we losing our kids?" was the nagging question. Not yet in middle school, their Jonathan was visibly drawn to television programs and movies that his friends were talking about all the time. The family had tried a couple of the movies, and had sat through the new sitcom that seemed to be so important to Jonathan. The smooth vulgar diet in language and plot line let them see how seducing the appeal was for Jonathan, especially under pressure to like what his friends like. Their daughter Jill is two years younger, and the stage is set for a parallel risk, with even greater visible consequences of exploitation if she buys into the peer and media hype as Jonathan seems to be doing.

Charlene and Roy, restless during the night, got up a little before 5:00 in the morning. "We are learning not to try to solve problems at night. They always seem more manageable in the mornings."

Before they awakened the kids to get them in motion for breakfast and to leave for school, Roy and Charlene savored a morning snack and asked themselves what they could do. Roy reported later that they decided to do something really different. "We realized that the problem was too big for us to solve alone. We've always said that God was out there to help us when we called. And we always offered table prayers before meals. Now, we decided that we needed to find out whether we really believed what we were saying. If so, we needed to bring God into this one big time!

"We decided to huddle with our kids at the front door and to add a prayer at their departure every morning. We would ask God to keep them and us from risky and dangerous things all day long as we mix with people and influences that may try to pull all of us away from what is good and true and consistent with the character of God."[1]

Now that Jonathan is 26 and Jill is 24, both are settled into productive adult lives and secure in their identities and life directions. Looking back, Charlene and Roy sigh, "Somehow it worked. We got honest about how destructive the workplace and school environments were, and our kids unhooked from the stuff they were buying into and took charge of their lives."

Now, let me describe what our single mom, Lorna, faced sometimes frantically. "I took my kids back!" Lorna now exclaims.

Lorna sat her Jan and Tim down after realizing that their demands for expensive fad clothing and entertainment were out of control and bankrupting them, even as the teens' unhappiness and demands seemed to increase. She also was feeling battle-weary from having to manage all of the adult load alone. She felt really alone, working, paying bills, and carrying the giant side of the home management work—laundry, cleaning, shopping, and preparing meals. She sprang her strategy on the kids this way:

"I want to make you kids partners. In just a few years you will be managing your own homes and families. Here's the bottom line on our week-by-week survival plan.

"Jan, I want you to open all of the bills and enter their amounts in the record book. All utilities go on this page. All monthly payments of store, gasoline, and other credit cards go on this other page. Jonathan, you can help Julie and learn how to make the entries. We're going to teach each other everything we know. You are going to show me how much you can carry of the adult load around here. Just think of it. In only a few years both of you will be up and out of the house and into your own careers, so I want to teach you everything I know

<hr />

[1]This story is based on one reported in their study of 3,000 families. See Nick Stinnett and John De Frain, *Secrets of Strong Families.* New York: Little, Brown, and Co., 1985.

about managing a home. Let's make use of the little time we've still got with each other so both of you will learn how to run your adult lives and be good at it.

"Here, on this page is where we will list our income each month. You can see how much money I bank every two weeks. That goes here under 'Income.' And here is the page where we record everything we spend to keep our car running. When you have them entered, put the bills in this clipboard, and we'll sit down and you can write the checks.

"For now, I'll sign the checks. Eventually, as each of you gets the hang of how to do this and do it well, we'll need your signatures on the account so either of you can handle our business for us. But you can see that we've got to have enough coming in to meet the expenses, or we are going to be in big trouble. You can watch the bank balance in the ledger section of the checkbook. That is the 'cushion' of money available. We need to keep about one month of my earnings in the cushion. But you can see how spending more for the house, the car, or for us, can reduce the cushion. If that happens, we could be driven to go and borrow money, then the interest starts eating us up. You'll notice that we pay our credit card bills before they become overdue and cripple us with high interest charges. With what we've got, we need to manage pretty carefully."

Then Lorna turned to Tim. "Tim, are you ready to manage the supervision of the house itself? This is what we need. Here is a clipboard we'll keep by the phone. We'll all use it to record messages we take for each other, complete with who to call back and what the number is.

"Let's use the same clipboard for your notes to us about what repairs we need to make anywhere on the property. And can you do an afternoon check on all rooms to see whether they are picked up and orderly? Let's make it our rule that each of us will take care of making the bed and hanging everything in its place, so nobody would be embarrassed if you or I had a relative or guest who dropped in on us. OK? If you'll monitor that, then make a note here about how well we are doing or what needs to be picked up, you'll do a wonderful and encouraging thing for all of us.

"One more thing about the clipboard. Will you monitor the family laundry schedule and suggest how we can get freshly clean clothes back in our bedrooms as soon as they are dry? If you see a way to organize collecting and sorting the laundry and get it in and out of the machines, tell us. You will make a fine gift to us if you can smooth that schedule and scheme out for us. And we will all share in the laundry routine. Drudgery is for sharing."

## Reading the Culture's Signals

Zachary Stone turned nine on December 1 a few years ago. His father, Lawson, my colleague, an expert in Old Testament interpretation, told me that he had realized that Zachary is ripening, and that it is a little scary when you see what happens to kids in their teens.

"I realized that I really needed to get to the kid before the craziness around us gets to him. So I asked myself what Zachary really wanted that would lift him on tiptoe toward more manly feelings and definitely more manly responsibility.

"One of the things Zachary had been begging for was a Swiss army knife. I'd been putting him off, telling him he wasn't ready for that, that it was potentially dangerous, and all of that.

"But it dawned on me that his ninth birthday might be just the right time to present it, complete with a letter welcoming him to his new domain upon entering manhood. I definitely wanted to get there first with that message. So I wrote him a letter and we gave him the Swiss army knife.

"When Angie and I gave him his special present, he opened it carefully and eagerly. My letter was the first thing he saw, but the box was obviously a Swiss army knife box. Zachary raced through the letter and quickly got to the business of handling the knife. So we let him open it up and exclaim his happiness! Then together we read the letter to him aloud and told him we would put the letter in his special drawer so he could read it again and again."

Here is a copy of Professor Lawson Stone's letter, furnished to me because of our common commitment to high quality family relationships:

December 1, 1994

Dear Zachary:

This is a big day in your life. You are nine years old. You are in third grade. You are still a boy, but you are also beginning the journey to manhood. I am very happy to see how you are growing up. I think you will become a fine man one day.

A real man has a man's body, mind, and spirit. Your body is getting bigger and stronger. Your voice is more commanding. More important, your mind is growing. You are learning *how to learn*. You are beginning to understand the *reasons* for our family beliefs and rules. Someday you will be free to make your own beliefs and rules because you will understand life.

Most important, in your spirit you are beginning to understand how important it is to take care about *others*, their safety, and their feelings.

This is a hard thing. Many boys never learn to take care of others. They grow up and even grow old, but they never become true men. This is still hard work for you, but I believe you are on the way.

In many countries, boys who are starting the journey towards manhood receive gifts from their fathers. The gifts are symbols of the goal—true manhood.

Jewish boys must learn to read the Bible in Hebrew and to lead in family prayers, so they receive a Bible and a special cloth to cover their heads when they pray. One group of African boys receives a small club called a *rungut*. It is a symbol of the job of being a leader. In other countries, boys are given their first real tools to use in their job. In early America, boys were given their first hunting tools.

You have a Bible, and I hope you will soon discover the deep secrets of prayer. You also have received tools and have begun working with them.

Today, I give you a very special gift on your journey to manhood. This is not just a present you are finally old enough to have. In giving this, I am telling you we believe in you. You have a long way to go. But you are becoming a fine man. This gift is also a test. It is dangerous. It can hurt, even kill. A man must learn to master dangerous tools and to use them for the good of other people.

The most important thing about becoming a man is something that neither Mother nor I can give you. A true man must not only have a man's body, mind, and spirit. A real man also must have Jesus as *his own personal Savior*. He must have a burning desire to *please God*, not because Mom and Dad want their son to please God, but because he has a powerful, burning faith in Jesus, and walks with Jesus in obedience to his teachings. A true man must be filled with the Spirit of God.

Zachary, if we could buy this last thing for you, we would sell everything, even risk our lives, and present it to you. A walk with Jesus is something only you can choose for yourself. Hating sin and loving righteousness comes only from your choice. We will continue to teach you, encourage you, and pray for you. But responding to Jesus and choosing to live in obedience to Jesus must come from your own heart. Every time you use this Swiss army knife, ask yourself: *Am I becoming a true man? Am I living in obedience to Jesus?*

I celebrate with you today because I know someday you will be a true man of God.

> With all my love and prayers,
>
> Dad

## What Kids Want

Remember? If we only listen to what the kids beg for, we will miss their deep hungers. Jonathan, in the first story, was dipping into the values and language of the electronic entertainment and peer cultures. Those toxic beliefs rest on assumptions kids buy from the propaganda in our culture, and then they imitate the behaviors, endorse them, and feed these toxic behaviors and lies to each other. Here they are again:

1. Adults work and sweat and are the most boring humans on the planet. But kids have all the fun, live to play, and their lives are exciting. Therefore, walk over your adults. Insult them. Deceive them. Humiliate them into doing what you demand. They are dumb. They don't get it, and if they have any feelings, it doesn't matter. They really want you to be happy, so you're actually treating them this way for their own good. Their entire reason for living is to meet kids' needs and provide everything they want—devoted to their kids' extravagant consumption and display demands.

2. Kids have a right to a free ride. Parents are easily shamed into furnishing a "limo" lifestyle by which the kid can indulge in extravagant consumption of goods, entertainment, privileges, and fad clothes, foods, and beverages.

3. Adults feel guilty because they work so many hours—partly to fund the teens' extravagant lifestyles—so a little begging and pouting will turn on the pressure that gets you anything you want.

Do you recall the diagram on "Rites of Reincorporation" from chapter 2? Without exception, kids who are launched into effective adult vocation always pass through a downhill, low point "liminal phase" before they are exalted and empowered as adults. The peak is the "rite of reincorporation" or transformation of the child into a visibly changed adult.

Here is a modified diagram I've sketched to show that in our culture with its toxic "adolescence," we have virtually guaranteed that our young will postpone embracing their adult vocation as long as possible. They are riding high when the "liminal phase" needs to be their curriculum. This "low point" phase is driven by the kid's desire to embrace adult reality and responsibility and by the family's faithfulness in scheduling and executing the empowering ritual of exaltation, release, and honored adult status.

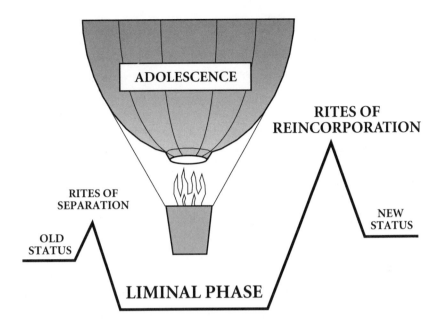

## RITE OF PASSAGE STRUCTURE

*Adapted from Zahniser, chapter 2. The "fire-driven balloon" suggests our "sacrifice" of our young on the altar of extravagant indulgence and of their extravagant consumption, and is reminiscent of the account of King Ahaz: "Ahaz made his son pass through the fire, according to the custom of the Gentiles whom God had destroyed" (2 Kings 16:3, paraphrased).*

Notice that this drawing suggests that our invented toxic adolescence comes at great cost. If parents try to buy their kids' favor or try to shield them from taking full responsibility for the family and for their own choices, we can set off a deceptive and extravagant "adolescence" which shoots them sky high. What the kids need, instead, is to work with the sobering facts of the real human world and their place in it. Ironically, this effort to shield or to indulge them results in burning up the family's resources to power this temporary high ride. Then, they in turn tend to be consumed or scarred for life as they stagger forward, dealing with the effects of their destructive adolescent lifestyle, and seriously impaired for productivity, peaceable adult careers, marriages, homes, and families.

The artificial high of the teen years easily becomes addictive, predicting that the emerging adult will see no way to support the lifestyle to which they have become accustomed. They will expect to have abundant time to devote to personal indulgence and full social agendas. They expect to have unlimited funds to purchase plush housing, abundant goods and expensive activities and privileges. Families which feed these self-indulgent, compulsive addictions to extravagance may be fueling the flames which keep this fragile balloon aloft in its artificial high. And if schools, churches, and other agencies have programs based on the assumptions of toxic adolescence endorsed everywhere in our culture—assumptions which feed on extravagant spending and fast-lane activities—the whole community is held hostage to the adolescence that is destroying us. If we plan events which indulge every whim with opulent trips and feed the kids directly into the flames of the electronic and advertising media, then ministers, teachers, and other mentors have unwittingly contributed to creating the destruction and chaos turned loose around us, and we all are losers.

When you read the developmental map called The Beatitudes which Jesus offered in the Sermon on the Mount, it is striking that it begins with poverty, both in the Matthew and Luke reports. I have arranged a summary of the eight developmental steps in the life pattern open toward positive and holy goals. But I was troubled from 1969 to 1985 when I was immersed in research in moral reasoning because none of the researchers were focusing on the immoral development that is evident all around us. So if you have wondered how two affluent kids from Littleton, Colorado, turned on their schoolmates

---

> 8 Advocates of 1, 2, 3
> 7 Peacemakers
> 6 Pure in heart
> 5 Merciful
> 4 Righteous/just
> 3 Meek/abused
> 2 Mourners/grieving
> 1 Poor
>
> ---
>
> One way of searching for the "mirror image" of morality might be to look for descending lists. Another would be to infer the negative side of the trajectory from the gradients on the positive side which is put forward. An interesting inversion occurs when we infer from the eight Beatitudes, since the first three appear to be negative. This will require what appear to be positive conditions for the first three of the potentially negative set.
>
> ---
>
> 1 Wealth
> 2 Ecstasy
> 3 Exaltation
> 4 Confrontation/demands for rights
> 5 Exploitation
> 6 Conspiracy/evil imagination
> 7 Anarchy
> 8 Terror

and a teacher on a spring day in 1999, gunning down thirteen of them in a few minutes and then killing themselves, brood over the "degenerative journey" map of inverted beatitudes here. I once called them the "ugly-tudes." And when you look at what happens to pampered, indulged, spoiled children in your neighborhood, the opposite trajectories here may offer some clues.[2]

If you look inside the child you work with, however, a deep cry for order, constraint, discipline, and adult empowerment emerges. What kids really want are simple and abundantly available gifts all parents can provide: wisdom, patiently developed and disciplined competency, effectiveness in relationships, and a sense of identity in the search for vocation and purpose in living. When parents meet those deep hungers consistently, the symptomatic behaviors of whining and demanding extravagant things tend to disappear. Look at those deep yearnings:

1. *A need to experience the value of being "blessed."* Parent signals and messages that the kid is a non-renewable, once-in-eternity gifted human bestows a gift of security at the core of those magical senses of role, status, value, and responsibility. When bestowed, this blessing and affirmation from the family produces a sense of optimism, security, and deep trust that the world works right. This deep peace and self-confidence grasps the truth that relationships are the ultimate source of identity and energy—not possessions and fads which cater to substances which are consumed in the body. Self-esteem is not a painted on or macho look, but an "inside job" distilled from abundant external readings in a full spectrum of real life connections and relationships.

2. *A sense of competency* derived from patient hard work and experience in learning, one-by-one, every skill the parents know:

   A. How to cultivate and establish a lifelong exclusive bond with a spouse, and the persistence to work through the tough responsibilities of love, marriage, and parenting.

   B. How to develop relationships of respect and trust with one's children and larger family network.

   C. How to argue a point without attacking a person.

---

[2]See my chapter, "Some Critical Adaptations for Judeo-Christian Communities," in Sohan and Celia Modgil's *Lawrence Kohlberg: Consensus and Controversy.* London: Falmer Press, 1985. The illustration here is reproduced from that chapter.

D. How to become independent in the use of household and personal equipment.

E. How to cope with strangers and aliens from the world of hype and extravagant consumption.

F. How to analyze advertising and popular myths from the electronic media to expose their real agendas and the real outcomes of their fantasy plots.

When these competency skills are developing, your children will become dialogic partners. They will also be displaying the early competencies and developing skills in the outer and often alien world of the popular culture. You will have cultivated the best survival skills on earth: the ability to maintain boundaries between the self and the outer world. "Remnant" and "conserving subcultures" are essential for the survival of the culture in which they struggle to maintain a sane identity while the culture is coming apart. Welcome to the world of creative, conspiring survivors and evangelists—witnesses of really good news.

3. *A grasp of the kid's own future,* including a timeline with marker points at which increased competency and demonstrated skill guarantee the open gates to wider options and additional choices. Parents, ministers, and other mentors can fuel the child's imagination of future destiny, of bridges to take him beyond this trap-point in the peer culture. Such vision and imagination can break the spell of the nonsense which suggests there is no tomorrow, so grab all the gusto today. Your kids will know that the ultimate and lasting ecstasy of freedom and responsibility are even now coming into view.

4. *A feeling that responsibility is increasingly theirs,* resting on their own shoulders. Children who experience irretrievable increments of responsibility interpret it to mean authority in small personal issues. They are affirmed to think that they are remarkably able to handle adult decisions by the mid-teens. While the consequences are small and nonfatal, children need to bail themselves out of a bad use of the week's money or reflect and suffer the consequences of the high cost of some childhood extravagance.

## What Parents Fear

How do you spell relief in the fast lane of parenting today? Very often we, like our kids, reach for some temporary and poor solution because we are harried, fatigued, and frustrated. Besides, in our worst insecure moments we are afraid that our kids will embarrass us and tarnish our carefully monitored image of being a happy family who has it all together. Try listing your fears and feelings which lead to ineffective parenting patterns. Here is a starter list:

1. We feel guilty because we work such long hours and cannot spend significant time with the children.

2. We feel sorry for the kids, under pressure to be liked by those all-time-most-important-people-in-the-universe: their peers.

3. We feel poor compared to the extravagance of our neighbors in outfitting their kids with every power symbol of the popular culture.

4. We want our kids to have more things, to enjoy more luxury, and thus feel more valued than we did as kids.

5. We would rather silence our child or buy him off by caving in to each demand than to open a conversation about his deeper hungers and needs.

## What You Deserve

Guess what? If you are a parent who dips into the depressing scenarios of feeling like an ineffective parent, know that you are one of millions suffering from this parent overload sensation. You deserve to locate a safe haven where you can conspire positively with other people who care about your child—a minister or other potential mentor for your kids—and find a place to be honest about your fears and failures. What I know about you is this: At a very deep and consistent level, I know that you have a hunger to find good characteristics in your kids and the eyes to give you hope that your kid is basically one

1. Who visibly glows with maturity when affirmed or blessed.

2. Who is relaxed and confident when contemplating becoming an adult.

3. Who speaks easily about a vocational dream and plans of how to get there.

4. Who has been seasoned for full responsibility by suffering the consequences of relatively small experimental losses suffered from poor choices.

On the other hand, if you are nervous, even scared at the thoughts of what your kid is coming to,

1. If your kid seems on edge, and restless and secretive about everything—

2. If your teen is in a compulsive demand mode and you are helplessly dispensing goods and services which are pampering every whim—

Then you may be ready to take the risk of getting honest with the child, to face your own fears, and to create a family system where everybody wins.

## The Deal Where Everybody Wins

You are the parents, the seasoned adults in this scenario. So look at the opening stories of parents in very different situations who decided to "upstage toxic adolescence," or "take back their kids" who were already in the grasp of the culture's magnetic pull. Decide whether, when, and how you will break the news to your kids that you have two pieces of good news.

1. The first chunk of good news is that you think you have figured out what it is that the kid really wants. Earl H. Gaulke wrote a book long ago entitled *You Can Have a Family Where Everybody Wins!*[3]

2. The second piece of good news is that you have a plan. You are going to bring your children on board as partners. You will coach them to prepare them for the day which is coming down the pike when they will be able to enter the adult responsibility scene and handle it well.

---

[3]Earl H. Gaulke, *You Can Have a Family Where Everybody Wins: Christian Perspectives on Parent Effectiveness Training.* St. Louis: Concordia, 1975. Dr. Gaulke wrote the book mostly for Missouri Synod Lutherans as a Christian presentation of core concepts in Thomas Gordon's *Parent Effectiveness Training: The Tested New Way to Raise Responsible Children.* New York: Peter H. Widen, Inc., 1970.

Find a way to share how good it is to unlock for them the secrets of the adult world; guarantee no secrets in response to their curiosity or their questions. Everything from bank balance and bills, from household management to auto maintenance, from tips on how to cope with acne to how to cope with sexual hunger and energy are all open for consultation as friends.

Then do something for yourself to keep your nerve up and your ideas coming. Huddle with other parents. Take *Empower Your Kids!* to your club, class, or church, and offer to convene a support group for parents ready to create empowering households and to drive the fear and darkness of the culture back out to the curb. Grab a copy of my *Risk-Proofing Your Family* and check for even more details about carving out hope and a good future for everyone dear to you, and share it with a group of parent friends. Ministers and other mentors will know these and other resources to encourage you in your bright adventure.

Take the list of things kids really want and rehearse as parents how you are going to usher in a new relationship with your kids. If you are a single parent, or a parent who must change the course of history while you still have opportunity with kids at home, rehearse in front of a mirror—much as you would pray and accept God's presence as your Master Guide in this parenting adventure. Next, phone your minister or other mentor who serves you and your kids, and ask for a "good conspiracy" to widen the circle of participation and support as you resolve to build a fresh and solid relationship with your kids. Try this: Phone another parent who is likely as frightened as you are about the future for your children. Share your discoveries and rehearse your plan. Customize the list below to describe your child's deep yearnings. See whether you can describe your own dream of empowering and releasing your child into full adulthood with those needs met:

## What Kids Really Want

1. A secure sense of being valued, loved, taken seriously, and trusted.

2. A confidence in his own competence to cope with anything that comes along.

3. A comfortable assurance that the future is there and that it is good—that the parents will be the front row cheerleaders in the stands and will be ready to leap onto the field in the event of injury but never to "make the play."

4. A poised sense of responsible power with freedom to make decisions whose consequences are within the range of risk and suffering the kid can handle.

In this chapter, I wanted to offer you both encouragement and strategies for seeing your kids as partners and friends in their adventure into adult responsibility and competence. It is significant, surely, that Jesus the Teacher transformed the "servant" disciples into friends on the simple principle I've offered here:

"No longer do I call you servants," Jesus said, "for a servant does not know what his master is doing." Then he continued, "But I have called you friends, for all things that I heard from My Father I have made known to you."

Double check the story line that begins in chapter 13 of John's Gospel, in which Jesus calls the disciples servants and accepts the title of Teacher. Then in chapter 15 (verse 15 is quoted above), Jesus actually turns those servants to friends. Finally, in his prayer for all who believe on him, Jesus strikes the mysterious Trinity chord in John 17: "that they all may be one, as You, Father, are in Me, and I in You; that they also may be one in Us..." (v. 21, NKJV). Sit back, then, and reflect on Jesus' promise to those children of his: "...greater works than these [you] will do, because I go to My Father" (John 14:12, NKJV). Odd, isn't it, that this progression is exactly what every parent, minister or mentor with your child wants to happen over a deliberate sequence, with high participation by the protégé, the emergent new adult.

If your household and your community get this kind of good conspiracy going, you truly will have a family in which everybody wins.

# 7

# Seeing the "Image of God" in Your Kids

I was empowered to marry, assume a two-state leadership job in coordinating teen ministries, and accept ordination with its authority to preach the Word of God—all in the year before I turned twenty.

For more than 40 years I have worked with families and teens. I have worked in the roles of both minister and mentor to hand over empowerment to emerging adults. I cannot imagine a more fulfilling calling and career than to have been given a ticket to watch hundreds of them come into full bloom by their mid-teens, then to welcome them into my world as colleagues and peers. I am hopelessly committed to this parenting, grandparenting, ministering, mentoring mission with teens, college people, and students in final preparation for careers in ministry.

Long before I could have helped you to see the image of God that is clearly visible in your kids, I was aware I was standing on the edge of a wonderful mystery. I occasionally stopped breathing as I watched the erupting energy of teens or was given a glimpse of their tentative stretching toward responsibility as they longed to embrace full adult powers.

These days my cup is full, as grandchildren are appearing on the adult screen, ready to step across the threshold to join their parents and grandparents as partners in adult status and responsibility. Already two of them have presented us with great-grandsons!

A few years ago at a family retreat in southern New York, I spoke to a young teenager I had not met before. I was teaching a parenting seminar all week, and he was in the separate youth program. But we faced each other in the slow-moving lunch line where the U-turn had us meeting virtually face-to-face and shoulder to shoulder. His cheeks were tinted with the vital coloring of his new maturity, and his face had recently been scraped clean by its first razor. Our eyes connected for a moment, and I spontaneously seized an opportunity to say aloud what struck me about the young man:

"Has anybody ever told you that you are dangerously good looking? If you don't give it all to Jesus, you are in big trouble!" I blessed him with an energized compliment.

This six-foot-tall kid leaned forward to respond in a forceful whisper. In his high animation, I could feel the puffing of his breath into my face; "There's this girl here who keeps following me around saying she wants to date me!"

"Do you see what I mean? You'd better give it all to Jesus now!"

His mother, who was in my parenting seminars each morning, tracked me down that evening. "You really made my son's day," she said, glowing.

"How did I do that?" I inquired innocently. I had not seen her with any children in tow. Then she quoted my words from the lunch line. "He came and told me as soon as I came in for lunch."

## God's Trinity Image to Us

The Judeo-Christian vision tells us that God fixed it so no one could get on this planet without exposure to the image of God. The Creation text (Genesis 1:27) states the source of this image of God stamped on the planet: God created them male and female, in God's image and in God's likeness. So one male parent plus one female parent comprise this image of God for children and for all who come in contact. Parents image God, not because they choose to do so, perhaps. Parents image God because they can't help it. Being present to the kid reveals God to the kid.

As a parent you spontaneously project images of God's character all around your kid. Mothers beam those divine characteristics which are reflected in "mothering." Fathers glow with those essential divine polar opposites representing the God of Old Testament power—nicely visible in images of spontaneous father behavior. A father's blessing of justice and protection or a mother's always embracing love, encompassing cradling, or engrossing playing, portray opposite but comprehensive dimensions of God's character. Continue the list: a father's preoccupation to provide or a mother's apparent instinct to nurture; all of them portray something about the character of God. What is more awesome is that half of the characteristics come spontaneously, but the other half become work for a single parent of either sex who may have to find a way to represent both ends of this spectrum of God's nature.

The marriage of a woman and a man, in a similar way, represents the mystery of the Trinity: "Three-are-one" in essence, one nature. They dwell together in holy community. So the yearning to look for love, to establish community, and to unite in producing a child which proceeds from the father and from the mother are Trinity imprints on human identity. The earliest Christian teachers saw the Trinity reflected in the family. "Look at your breakfast table," Gregory of Nazianus would preach. Then he would unfold the following logic, first using the Trinity as a model for family relationships, then using the family as a means of understanding the mystery of the three-in-one Holy Trinity. Here is his teaching in summary: "Consider the mystery of the Holy Trinity—Three Persons in One. Look no further than your breakfast table. Your family is an image of the Holy Trinity. There is the Father. There is the Mother. There is the Child. They are one. They are of the same essence. The Child proceeds both from the Father and from the Mother, yet is distinct from each. They are three persons, yet they are one. So the Holy Trinity consists of Father, Son, and Holy Spirit who live in Holy Community."[1]

So all human yearning for intimacy and union is a God-driven appetite to establish an image of the Trinity. Your babies will grow up to follow the same yearnings, partly because of how you have represented God to them, but mostly because God re-invents the image of God in every daughter and son. "In the image of God, male and female" is God's continuing world witness to represent the core dimensions of the character of God.

The amazing truth is: our kids sense the wonder of sexual ripening and hear the voice of God saying, "This is very good! Your best ripening maturity is my image speaking to you about me!" So the impact on your kids as they hit puberty is a profound double assault. Now I ask you, why would God load into a kid's sexuality and reproductive potentials the hunger to know God, to discover meaning and purpose, and to consummate ultimate Trinitarian unity in a sexual relationship that can produce that third-dimension child you long to see? So if you have teens emerging around the house, or if God has

---

[1]See Jürgen Moltmann's summary of Gregory of Nazianus' homilies in *The Trinity and the Kingdom*. SCM, 1981.

trusted you with ministry with youth, or if you are someone these hungry young adults trust, know this:

1. Your teen will have a deep sense and hunger to "find the other," the yearning to be one with another human of the other sex. I call this the Trinitarian hunger, because each of us seems to be born knowing that we are created for exclusive attachment, that there is a missing "other." Love, marriage and sexual union are the ritual components of each journey to create a fresh Trinity image.

2. The sexual ripening at pubescence is accompanied by the completion of the myelinization of the correlation fibers of the central cortex. With this reflection capacity now in service, each kid can ask ultimate questions, "Where did I come from?" "What am I here for?" "Where am I going?" and "Where will I find someone to whom to reveal my dream and tell my secrets?" "Is it possible that there is someone out there to love me forever?"

Fasten your seat belts, and look at these and other ways God's image is written in your kids' sexuality and in sexual identities as male or female.[2]

## Gift of Being a "Person"

OK. You knew you created a new human being, a person. But personhood emerges slowly from the image of God in your kid. Paul Tournier in a wonderful book for parents, called *Secrets*, describes how the child is first enveloped in the parental identity.[3] Then, the child begins to hide away small personal objects, or perhaps the child tells an occasional "lie" to keep a part of personal knowledge secret.

Tournier says the child must have secrets to become an individual. He says that wise parents urge the child to have a secret place or a drawer or box with a lock and who respect the privacy of the growing child.

But no one becomes a "person" until the deep personal secrets are presented to someone else. Children's friendships by middle school revolve around secretive hideouts, giggling girls in a sleepover, or boys moving by stealth or

---

[2]Clifford Stevens, in his research report on the contamination of sexuality in the Western World, speaks eloquently about the image of God in human sexuality in "The Trinitarian Roots of the Nuptial Community." *St. Vladimir's Theological Quarterly*, Vol. 35, No. 4, 1991. Lawrence Friesen, in a doctoral dissertation completed at Fuller Theological Seminary, arrives at the same judgment against Western Christianity for having contaminated human sexuality. Trace his historical and biblical analysis in Lawrence Friesen, *Sexuality: A Biblical Model in Historical Perspective*. Pasadena Fuller Theological Seminary, Doctor of Ministry dissertation, 1989.

[3]Paul Tournier, *Secrets*, translated by Joe Embry. Richmond: John Knox Press, 1965.

building a tree house to get away. There are trips to the attic or garage to display for a special audience the objects stowed away as "my secrets."

Tournier notes that eventually the emerging young man or young woman will take strength and confidence from sharing secrets in teen years with a confidential few. They are now quite sure that the risk of falling in love and trusting one solitary person is worth taking. They search deep interior secret places where fears and past regrets are filed away. Then they begin to reveal secrets no one else has heard. They are nervous, but know that truth and shared secrets are necessary to build a life together based on absolute trust. So they invite this prospective life companion as if to confide: "I want you to know everything about me, including some things no one else knows and some things I wish I did not have to reveal. But I could not bear to have you learn any of these things from someone else."

Loneliness is such a marker of God's Trinity imprint that emerging adults and humans all through life are wise to follow the yearning which cries out to take the risk of establishing one or two confidential relationships, if only with peer mentors. In those relationships they will be able to trust one or two people with deep life secrets. Jesus evidently knew this Trinity hunger to share with a small network of trusted confidants. He called away three apostles for special prayer agendas. And Jesus encourages us that "Where two or three of you are gathered in my name, there I am in the midst,"[4] suggesting a Trinitarian kind of community of trust.

Ultimately, Tournier observes, to become truly "a person" means giving all of one's secrets over to God. So marriage and confidential relationships, first with parents, then with ministers and other mentors, are sure to give us a high sense of "being truly human." But God, who knows us beyond verbal symbols, even the "deep groanings which cannot be uttered," is our best and complete Confidant. So we surrender, give up, and make a bold appeal for God to search our deepest motivations and longings and to find secrets which are hidden even from ourselves.

We rehearse our journey to personhood by beginning to share secrets in childhood with close friends. Then, many of us find the "other," both in

---

[4]Jesus took Peter, James, and John with him to the place of prayer. "My soul is overwhelmed with sorrow to the point of death," he said to them. "Stay here and keep watch" (Mark 14:34). The formula of "two or three, gathered" in the name of Jesus, as a guarantee that he will show up is recorded in Matthew 18:19-20: "...I tell you that if two of you on earth agree about anything you ask for, it will be done for you by my Father in heaven. For where two or three come together in my name, there am I with them."

mentors and in love and marriage. We will likely be seeking out mentors or spiritual directors our life long. But all of us can come with complete transparency before the God who created us, knows us anyway, and magnetically pulls us into intimacy of affection, worship, and lifelong communion.

God, who resides in holy community as a Person in relation to others, has created your daughter or son to achieve that remarkable point of dignity, of becoming a person, in this fullest sense. You are watching it happen, but your child will be investing the energy on the journey to individuation and to personhood. You can cheer and bless, but you cannot bestow personhood by yourself. So, when your kid hits a home run in reaching out for a new Trinity-like connection, and you sense that God's best has broken through to reveal the image feature of personhood, stand up and cheer.[5]

## Children as Sovereigns in Waiting

Not only are we created for relationships and for personhood, but the identity as person brings with it the God-like need for sovereignty. Sovereignty does not refer to ruling over others. To be a sovereign is to be a king or queen who manages the interior world: self-control, boundaries, and the ability to manage the self. Sometimes the so-called "strong-willed child" is seen as a threat in the family. But most often such a child needs discipline and empowerment to take full responsibility for choosing behavior that delivers the best consequences for the self. When your own or your child's sovereignty is secure and well disciplined, it is no threat to anyone and does not seek to be a rebel or to be disorderly. Quite the opposite; only a secure sovereign at peace with the inner kingdom is able to be peaceable with others.

This child of yours begins to show sovereignty when the need for secrecy and privacy appear. But blessing the sovereignty in a child also gives early and increasing responsibility for routine choices and tasks, and allows the little sovereign to suffer consequences for careless management of his or her "kingdom." It would have been easier for Dr. and Mrs. Mark Lee to have made the choice of shoes for their young daughter who sat surrounded by a half-dozen pairs of shoes at a store in the mall.

---

[5]For two remarkable books on personhood in the image of God, see *The Self as Agent* (1957) and *Persons in Relation* (1961). These John Macmurray titles were the Gifford lectures at the University of Glasgow, Scotland, in consecutive years, 1953 and 1954. Both are available (1978 and 1979), Atlantic Highlands, NJ: Humanities Press.

"You decide." She begged them to make the choice.

"But you will be the one to wear them, so you think about your favorite clothes and places you will be wearing them, and you decide. You are the person who can do that best."

Her parents then took a walk through the shopping mall, returning every ten minutes or so to find her still brooding over the choice she needed to make. But she exercised her little sovereignty and all lived happily most of the time— except when she remembered she could have had another pair of shoes instead of the ones she chose.

But Mark Lee, telling the story of their daughter's broken plans for a wedding, recalled the night she awakened her parents. At twenty-one she was planning a wedding, but the groom-to-be demanded sex "tonight, or the engagement is off." Painful as it was to take her fiance seriously, she told him simply, "I decided a long time ago I wasn't going to bed with anyone until I married him. So if that's your demand, the wedding is off."

"Sovereignty" as God's image printed in your kid will give the child a sense of (a) inner control, (b) outer boundaries, and (c) freedom to establish healthy relationships both in the family and beyond it. Children with no boundaries are vulnerable to exploitation everywhere. So by the time your child hits fifteen, you will want to know that there is a good track record in making sovereign decisions that wear well.

## Justice and Love Incarnate

"It's not fair!" is the first cry revealing the child has God's character image stamped deeply within. Steve and Sybil Wolin report in *The Resilient Self*[6] their discovery of seven characteristics they find in "resilient survivors." They assert that even those children who suffer from abuse are so powerfully created with an inner sense of justice that 60 percent of them "won't do anything as adults that even resembles abuse." The reason they don't buy into abuse seems to be related to the fact that they have insight. They know that something in the family isn't right, and they develop a way of coping with what is wrong without compromising their deep sense of righteous justice. They have an indestructible morality: they recognize the parents' abusive behavior as wrong.

If the child's sense of justice and morality were consistently surrounded by honesty and integrity in the family, we can only speculate how much higher

---

[6]See Steven and Sybil Wolin, *The Resilient Self: How Survivors of Troubled Families Rise Above Adversity.* New York: Villard Books, 1993.

their survival rates would be. Daughters, it turns out, organize their sense of integrity around issues of attachment and of what is right or wrong about relationships.

Carol Gilligan, whose work extends the research of Jean Piaget and Lawrence Kohlberg, reminds us of some intrinsic patterns of gender differences in her book *In a Different Voice: Psychological Theory and Women's Development.*[7] The gender differences are measured, as well, in Isabel Meyers' foundations for *Introduction to Type*[8] and other Meyers-Briggs personality profile assessment research. She finds that males by a 60-40 percent split are more likely to make decisions based on facts, and females by the same split are more likely to make decisions based on how people are impacted by the consequences.

Boys are more likely to look at events more objectively—from the outside— and to declare what is right and wrong, much as a referee would do. Boys are also much more likely to display their justice skills as standards held high to measure a person's performance as if by some eternal yardstick. A young man's perfectionism may drive the standard too high for himself and everybody else. A young woman, in contrast, is more likely to grieve over strained or broken relationships. Either pattern may appear in any man or woman. But both are evidence of God's image of justice and love stamped deep in the core of human personality.

Your kids' sense of justice will be a great encouragement to you as you release them into a world of risk and violated rights and values. And their sense of integrity will serve them well as they evaluate relationships, choose training options and careers, and carry a sense of righteous justice wherever they go. Eventually their usefulness to the world will be directly related to this root of justice and righteousness with which God endowed them, male and female.

## Ecstasy and Worship

You celebrated your naked newborns, upside down and wailing, as the physician announced "It's a girl!" or "It's a boy!" And when they were vulnerable and helpless, you bathed and dressed them. Then by age five you

---

[7]See Carol Gilligan, *In a Different Voice: Psychological Theory and Women's Development,* Cambridge: Harvard University Press, 1982. See also her more recent research report on young girls: *Making Connections: The Relational Worlds of Adolescent Girls.* Cambridge: Harvard University Press, 1990.

[8]Isabel Briggs Meyers, *Introduction to Type.* Gainesville, FL: Center for Applications of Psychological Type. See also David Kiersey and Marilyn Bates, *Please Understand Me.* Del Mar, CA: Promethean Nemesis, 1978.

tutored them in sense of privacy about covering their sexual bodies. But somewhere along the childhood road into the second decade of life, they almost inevitably discovered the special pleasures of sexual arousal. And with the awakening of the hormones and pheromones which push them into adult bodies comes the high alert for establishing a lifelong sexual relationship with one beloved partner. They were ready and eager to share their sexual secrets and to bring pleasure to an exclusive, life marriage partner.

The impulse to "couple" is deeply rooted in our humanity. God who is a person, who is sovereign, and who is righteous and just is also the one whose image is mysteriously represented by the magnetic and ecstatic pleasure of our sexual gifts and our sense of sexual identity.

It is appropriate to ask "How could sexual ecstasy 'image' the Divine Person to us humans?" But when you look at the world, exploding with extravagant splendor in springtime, summer, fall, and winter, you can easily conclude that each creative decree or gesture was accompanied by celestial ecstasy and joy. Those of us who spend weeks out-of-doors sense the nearness of God in the wonder of creation. And some of us have near "out of body" experiences of worship when we are at prayer or worshipping through music. Ecstasy as the "image of God," we may ask? But the linkages are clear: worship at its best is a celebration whose nearest equivalent is the ecstatic moment which the French call "*le petit morte*," the little death—full surrender to sexual loving. So sensuous pleasure may be the universal "image of God reminder" that our ultimate ecstasy comes in intimately knowing God.

## Trinity and Community

Finally, though the image of God characteristics may be an unending ledger of revelation through our sexual identity, your child will see God's mark on life as the awakening yearning for "community." The Creation dictum, "It is not good that the *adam* [the human] should be alone" is written deeply in the yearnings of every human being. So establishing confidential and intimate friendships during early pubescence becomes a burning need in the early adult years. Before landing the marriage covenant and intimacy, or throughout life for those who choose or are destined to celibacy and single-ness, the search is on. "Don't ask me to another 'all female' Sunday class!" Esther retorted. "I live alone with a female cat. I work in an office with six women. When I go to church I want to be where there are both men and women!" The deep yearning, of course, is that at the macro level there is a witness to the divine nature in every environment where men and women are spontaneously and elegantly present.

At the micro level, sexual intimacy is the motor driving falling in love, sharing the total inventory of confessed secrets, marrying and expressing sexual loving throughout a lifetime. A sort of ultimate hope is that in the consummation of sexual loving, they will be granted the privilege of creating new life that will inhabit eternity—children born of their celebration of a new community: man, woman, and couple. It is clear that this yearning for intimacy continues for life. Not long ago I alternated platform responsibilities in Gatlinburg, Tennessee, with Pastor Rosemary Brown. There were more than 5,000 teens assembled for three days. Late in the convention, Pastor Brown opened her evening address by saying, "I'm 57 years old, and I'm a virgin. I wouldn't have it any other way. But I have to tell you that there is scarcely a day goes by that I do not glance over my shoulder just in case my knight in shining armor is coming over the horizon." The teens fell into a breathless hush. They suddenly realized that the yearning is holy, and that it is not the sole domain of the very young.

In this chapter I wanted to display the crown jewel of human experience: the "community" need behind God's observation: "It is not good that the human should be alone." The "Trinity hunger," I sometimes call it, is associated with Trinity candles at weddings. "Two become one" and form a mysterious triad of wife, husband, and marital couple, eventually to become tangible in the extension of each—the child. Encourage your sons and daughters to leave all three candles burning during their marriage ritual. Male, female, and couple are magnificent witnesses of God's grand creation. The wedding celebrates the new creation: the couple. But man and woman continue as solid presentations of God's character. Gregory of Nazianus was onto something: There may be yet another Trinity mystery that will unfold for this new couple. Much like the Holy Spirit, who issues from the Father and the Son, forming the Holy Trinity, so also the child issues from the father and the mother to form the family. "Let them be one, even as You, Father are in Me and I am in You:" is the ultimate Trinity prayer for solidarity, unity, and common identity.

So you will want to be on the side of the angels when your young burst into full developmental "bloom" and they long to establish a new Trinitarian community. Celebrate the new image of the Trinity that they will come to represent—the most elegant of the "images of God" on earth.

# 8

# Empowering with Family Promises

"I promise God and I promise you, my parents, that I accept this ring as a symbol of my covenant from this moment to accept responsibility as an adult with full integrity. I will wear this ring on my right hand to remind me, and the woman that I may marry, that I promised at age 17 to be faithful to her from this moment for the remainder of my life. On my wedding day, I will present it to her as a necklace pendant, symbolizing my exclusive love."

John Mark was his parents' guest at his favorite restaurant. He thought the subject would be college, but his father and mother opened, instead, the subject of the signs of his sexual maturing, and the pleasure of watching his recent overwhelming experience of falling in love. They discussed the predictable delight of some day consummating marriage with the right woman, in the right time, and in the right way, and of living in joyful faithfulness to the good woman who would respond to his search for lifelong marriage.

Some time after that restaurant interchange, Mark Kennedy told me of his response to attending one of my seminars. "I was remarkably touched by your idea of the beautiful gold ring. Kathy and I talked about it when I returned from your rites of passage seminar. We went out looking for three identical wedding rings—one for each of our three teens. We booked John Mark's session on Monday evening and Joseph's on Tuesday. We'll wait for Sara to have her first period before scheduling a meal with her. We developed a parent-kid covenant for the restaurant ceremony from which the three of us read. The covenant culminated with our presentation of the gold ring.

"When we got home on Monday night, John Mark took off for his girl friend's house, wearing his ring and with his copy of the covenant in hand. One of their friends was there, too. John Mark told the story of the family covenant and the promises. 'They were impressed,' he told us later.

"With Joseph we knew we would have to get past his making a joke of the whole thing. That's his job in the family, to be funny and entertaining. We even rehearsed a couple of scenarios about how to get past the humor facade with Joseph. Once down to business—with our rehearsal of how we had conceived him to become a man, how pleased we were with who he had become in such a short time, only fifteen years—he sobered down into an amazing and responsible maturity. We told him that we wanted him to accept our gift of his own adult responsibility in exchange for wearing a covenant ring as a promise to his future wife. The ring would remind him of his promise to be sexually faithful to the woman he would present himself to on his wedding day. We suggested how he could develop a 'liturgy of presentation' that would become part of the marriage service for presenting the ring on a pendant necklace as the completed symbol of his fidelity.

"When we got down to reading the restaurant covenant from our three printed forms, Joseph carefully formed his words: 'I covenant with God and with you to live my entire life in keeping with the highest standards of honesty and integrity. I wear this ring as a symbol of this covenant.' We responded to his promise by reading, 'We covenant with God and with you, Joseph, to be a constant source of support and encouragement to you. We covenant to pray daily and without ceasing for you and for the woman God brings into your life. We will be praying that your life will be anchored in complete reverence for God and will be complete and exclusive with one another. We give this ring as your symbol of your covenant.'"

Mark and Kathy Kennedy report that both John Mark and Joseph have given their permission for the story of the family promises to be shared, first in Pine Forest, where they live and go to school, then beyond their community.

At the restaurant during Mark and Kathy's briefing on embracing full manhood and responsibility, Joseph reported that he had been put on the spot in ROTC only that week. "Anybody here still a virgin?" one of the teen boys had taunted. Two young women and Joseph had raised their hands. Joseph paid a price afterwards as some of the boys tried to humiliate him.

On Wednesday morning, after Joseph's covenant ceremony, he came through the kitchen sporting his ring. "Well, I've got my chastity belt on," he reported proudly, and was off to school.

## Identify the Hunger for Adulthood

Count on it. Your kids started out thinking you were like angelic beings or gods in their lives. You were invincible, always right, always strong, always confident, and always able to achieve your goals over impossible odds. None of those things were actually true. But the kids truly believed them and saw you as invincible giants.

As they grew and needed instruction and correction, your "credentials" of perfection served them and you very well. Now that they are going over the edge into adult bodies and into adult choices of all kinds, never forget that you were their first and best teachers and models.

If you level with them, they will learn now what they could not understand then: that big people are sometimes frightened, not always successful in achieving their goals, and have never been all-powerful or all-wise. They will have begun to suspect your imperfections, and are likely to hold you in mild disappointment or contempt if you still try to fake perfection, omniscience, and omnipotence now. But they will embrace an important part of their own adulthood as you level with them, even reporting specific episodes you wish you had handled better when they were younger.

When your kids catch you listening to them, eager to crack the code of their own culture's language and symbols, they will have become your teachers. My advice is that you never try to use their language, but that you use all sorts of questions to get inside and understand what the agendas and deep hungers are which drive the constant shift in fashions, art, and language. The message you are giving by such questioning is that you do not know everything, that roles are changing, and that they can teach you a good deal. This sets the stage for you to explore with them some of the deep truths and values that never change from one generation to another.

In the chaos of changing cultures, you will have watched longer and will have a sense of where important shifts are occurring. See whether you can sense some shifts for higher integrity and value. But push probing questions in the direction of eroding integrity and value issues. By the time your kid hits seventeen, the middle-school kids will look dangerous and crazy to that teenager of yours, compared to the thin four-year school cultural band. So embracing adulthood deserves some tools and skills for shaking down cultural shifts and for maintaining the unshakable foundations of integrity, honesty, and the common good for all.

In this "growing adulthood" portrayal, you are making adulthood look like an attractive and viable place to live—something now feared by many of our young. When Mark and Kathy empowered their sons in the restaurant liturgies of embracing their manhood, they also promised to "hang on" as friends and peers for the rest of their lives. We are fortunate indeed when the generations hang together across the ripple effect of changing cultural fads, values, and language.

## Shape the Promise

Your family has its own set of hopes and of "life marker points." Try to locate a few that have been handed down and ask whether they are worth preserving in family stories and in perpetuating family traditions. One very old tradition for young women was built around a hope chest, or a trousseau. This was a future bride's collection of adult clothing, linens, and other homemaker wares, many of them handmade by craftswomen in the extended family. In those older and typically rural generations, a future groom knew he was going to be launched one day as a man when a designated acreage was set aside for his production of marketable goods, and when seed livestock was given as a means for him to develop his own herd.

Today's families are more likely to open a trust account, which matures at a time to invest in the child's launching as an adult. Every affectionate and humane culture devises means for endowing their young and boosting them into an attractive, viable, and workable adult vocation. The families which disinherit the kids and send them out bankrupt or with a hundred thousand dollars of educational loans to repay are creating a frightened and hostile young adult population—whose rising "singles" numbers and perpetually self-indulgent adolescents are a visible result. This frightened, disinherited generation fears further responsibility just at the time their biological agenda demands that they pledge "all my earthly goods" to endow a solid future for the home and family. You will notice that thoughtful families today always find ways to perpetuate the endowed futures of their young.

## Choose the Symbols

Engagement rings and substantial wedding gifts are an American version of a dowry. The value of the stone becomes a down payment guaranteeing the financial and material security of the future career together.

We sometimes imagine that symbols stand for the real thing, but are only arbitrarily invested with meaning. But when symbols are invested with meaning through intentional naming or through a ceremony of presentation, the symbol actually participates in the event and becomes part of the reality.

John Mark's and Joseph's chastity promise rings will always denote their lifelong fidelity to one woman. If those rings were to be lost, no other ring they might acquire would symbolize the promises they made, because those rings were not "there" when the words were said, and hence lack the deep symbolic value of the original rings.

My own father was gathered with his four brothers around their Dad to hear his promise. My father would have been in his teens. "I want to tell you," my Grandpa Charles Wesley Joy said, "that today I have stopped using tobacco and profanity. I apologize to you for doing those things. You will never hear me swear or see me use tobacco again, because I've surrendered all of my life to Jesus. And if you will promise never to use tobacco or bad words, I will give you each a gold watch on your twenty-first birthday." You will not be surprised to learn that this piece of adult honesty with his sons established a relationship on which he delivered a gold watch to each of his sons.

Cedar chests, gold watches, and rings may be arbitrary at the time they are chosen, but those objects become holy through their association with the holy event in which they were presented. If I had inherited my father's white gold Elgin pocket watch today and could hold it or look at it from time to time, in holding it I would be revisiting the ceremony in which it was given on Dad's twenty-first birthday to denote a promise his father made and a promise my father kept. There is a pretty real sense in which that beautiful watch and its story account for my own resistance to the pull of the crowd to experiment with smoking. All of that covenant is now fully embedded in that one particular antique gold watch, making it an heirloom with a story worth keeping alive. I want you to sense that family ceremonies can become powerful ritual processes which take on a life of their own because they become associated with promises and objects held in memory.

Mark and Kathy combined a printed liturgy with a gold ring for their sons, and they suggested a presentation of the ring as a pendant on their wedding days. Those "promise rings" will be fused with the stories they represent, and you can expect to find them being passed on to children and grandchildren, along with the story of the family promises.

## Watch the Anticipation

Robbie and I did it intentionally. Our promise to our young sons came out of happy and thankful hearts and out of our uninhibited joy of watching them quickly growing up. The promise was made at breakfast. While we had agreed to make the announcement, we did not think of developing a written ritual or of presenting some token or symbol of the promise. John was ten and Mike was only six.

"We have a promise we want to make to you boys," we said. "On our wedding day, my parents gave us the new family car they had recently purchased. They told us at the wedding, and we drove the car on our honeymoon.

"So we've decided that we are going to do the same thing for each of you. You will get your new four-door full-sized Chevrolet on your wedding day or on the day you graduate from college, whichever event comes first."

Our little boys were delighted. From time to time they would banter, "Is a Corvette a Chevrolet? That's what I want, Daddy!" We delivered new Chevys to each son midway through the college journey. We think the way we framed the promise may have kept their minds on fidelity and marriage more than on wasting the college years in serial relationships.

I occasionally wondered whether we had made the promise too soon. Then, working as we did with teens in our church, we watched young men and cars destroy each other and blow up their futures. As our sons reached puberty and the approaching driver's license age, they seemed relaxed.

Harvest working trips to Grandpa Joy's Kansas farm saw John and then Mike licensed by the County Agent in Meade County. They were authorized to operate tractors, wheat combines and other motorized equipment, and they drove the pick-up and farm trucks in Kansas at the age of thirteen. But back in Indiana we saw not one sign of pushing to jump the gun and cheat by driving underage, before sixteen. They did not even push the limits by starting the car or by teasing us to let them drive it on our extensive paved driveway system at home. They were at peace. The day was coming when they would have a car. The early promise and patterns of delivery on family promises evidently defused the adolescent craziness we were seeing all around us. And both we and our sons were eager for the day when fully licensed drivers were added to the household resources to manage our full schedule of obligations all around.

"Let me tell you why this is important for us," I said. "My parents gave us our first car, and it meant that we didn't have to make payments, that we could travel home across country from college in Illinois, and that it wasn't a worn-out junker needing constant repair. That was such a blessing to us. So, we decided we are going to pass the blessing on to you."

Not until my parents' last years did I learn the rest of the story. Their gift to us was a second-generation transformation of a gift they had received from Mother's parents. My Indiana-based Royer grandparents had determined to furnish each son with a team of fine horses as a wedding gift. The horses were essential to farming and doubled as fine stock for transportation as well. So when mother married, Grandpa Royer told my father that since he came out of Kansas, a team of horses would be hard to move from Indiana to Kansas. Besides, tractors were replacing horses both in Indiana and Kansas. So Grandpa David Quillow Royer presented the marrying couple with a cash gift equal to the value of a fine team of horses and suggested that they buy a car. They did, and now additional generations are continuing the ritual process.

## Deliver the Goods

Remember Jason's excitement before he was two when I outlined the manly work we would do together when we got to "Mamaw's house"? I told the whole story in chapter 1. Empowering promises transform the kids. Families have a "prediction" factor. Children's memories are recorded in their nerve endings and in the fabric of their personalities. Trust is established as they find their needs consistently met in the first year of life. When they find that the world actually treats them well and meets their needs, kids learn that dreams do come true—that basic needs of meals and holidays and Christmases actually do turn into promised realities.

Children whose basic infant needs were not met, or around whose head a world of safety and security has come crashing down, may no longer be sure about promises and dreams. It is never too late to tell the truth and to invite a dream, and to start over in building a sense of trust and hope in a kid. Getting them through the years between ten and twenty is greatly simplified if they can be sure that although there are miles to go, there are promises worth keeping and glorious days of delivery awaiting them.

Well, in this chapter I've handed over the empowering "gold" if you are ready to invest intentionally and powerfully in your kids. Parents and grand-parents provide the linkage to the kid's future—a solid and smooth inheritance of resources: values, beliefs, and collected traditions and family wealth. One solitary family can swim upstream against the current and the masses drifting the other way. But agencies such as churches, congregations, and other social systems can greatly enhance the family if clusters of households form a common vision and strategize together. Eventually, a whole community might create an environment in which families find wide support in bucking the tide of destructive adolescent cultural patterns.

In chapter 9 we turn to celebrate the supreme leverage when communities initiate. Ritual processes established as visible community rites of passage, delivered by community authority, can greatly widen the network of holiness and safety in our troubled world.

# 9

# Initiating Kids
# Through Community Rites

Frankly, I had no idea that Kip was being transformed by his week of rugged trail camping with us. Greg was one of three graduate students in ministry who coordinated life for the trail family that included Kip and four other teen men. I mention Greg because it was clear from the first day that Kip was energized by being around Greg. Greg played guitar for the group activities each evening, and his easy leadership style and friendly laughter evidently were part of the magnet that pulled Kip into adoring Greg as mentor and model.

Almost a year after Kip spent that week in Greg's trail family, I got a call inquiring whether Kip's father could register for the trip. His pastor reported that the father wanted to be in the same trail family with his son, if that were possible. I'm a pretty congenial professor, so the trail families the next year included Robert Newell and his son Kip. The pastor also reported that Robert is a remarkably good man, but not a believer. "He grew up in a pastor's family. But we only see him in church with his wife and children on Christmas and Easter."

At the trailhead Rob introduced himself to me. "I can't wait to see what you do to these kids," he began. "Last year we hardly knew Kip when he came home. I figured that you did some kind of magic with him. He came home eager to cooperate, to take responsibility everywhere. I know he went to visit some of the extended family, and they later told me that they couldn't believe how Kip had changed."

Robert found out that very day. The first evening's "tarp talk" agenda to wind up the trail family's first hike was a bombshell for Kip's dad. After his trail family counselor-mentor had introduced the life-story agenda and provided a window into himself, he threw it open to the teens. Kip volunteered to go first. The starter stem the new seminary minister had announced was simple: "If you want to know who I am, you need to know that the most important thing that has happened to me in the last year has been...." The challenge the seminary student threw out was to complete the sentence he had just completed.

"Well," Kip volunteered, "if you want to know the most important thing that has happened to me during the last year, it was what happened on this trip a year ago. I discovered that I really wanted to get my whole future organized around Jesus, so I just turned it all over to God. I did it here. Greg was one of my trail family counselors last year. He became my instant hero that week. I saw in Greg exactly the kind of man I wanted to become. When I got home, I had to go around to several folks and straighten some things out, because I had really left a lot of tracks acting like an irresponsible jerk. So I apologized and some of that was very hard, but everything else has been worth it. This has been the best year of my life!"

When the week of trail camping wound down, Rob reflected on the surprise of Kip's revelation about a moral and religious transformation. "I'm going home with more questions than I had when I arrived," Rob told me.

I encouraged Rob. Facing mid-career as he was, I congratulated him on the increasing complexity of his questions. Mid-life often shakes out the best— or sometimes the worst—in a man. "Ask all of your questions," I said. "And when you are ready, I'm ready to walk with you through any kind of questions that trouble you."

That was July, and in January, Robert brought his questions, along with a longstanding cynicism and agnosticism. In my office we had a five-hour exchange that left a deep impact on both of us. We owed that exploration into God's grace to his young son's fascination and empowerment by a young mentor in the trail family exchanges of a week on the Sheltowee Trace of Daniel Boone National Forest.

You can imagine that the Kip-Greg-Robert empowerment saga gave me a full cup of reflection across the next few years. By about ten years later, I had collected more human development research. And I decided to get more intentional in setting up this "mentor-minister-parent-kid" experience to see whether the transformation could occur predictably with more intentional planning. Finally, I challenged a fresh crop of YM 690 graduate students to create a "rites of passage" week for teens and parents. Three of the larger team of a dozen actually designed and wrote the curriculum and the ritual for the surprise "rite." We scheduled the climactic ritual for the fifth night in the Red River Gorge.

## A Summer's Passage: Toward Freedom and Responsibility

As we do every summer, we formed a half-dozen trail families of eight into groups which included three graduate students, three parents, and their three teens. We wanted to bring parents into the ritual process as we empowered their own teens to become adults. Four of the teens registered were without a parent on the trip, so we anticipated a mentor would emerge from my students as the week unfolded. I further briefed my students on pre-registration facts about their assigned teens, noting special handicapping conditions or medical needs. We had separate trail families for women and for men.

The curriculum design included two informal daily experiences. The first each day was a 10:30 a.m. "Trail Break" conversation focused on high priority teen issues and concluding with a Scripture "rap" to hammer home a resource for the teen issue.

The second informal event was structured at the end of the day, in the darkness under the trail family's tarp. We use no enclosed tents, but community-size 24' x 20' tarps open on both ends and rigged with one high open side and one low open side for ventilation. Distance between tarp sites provided adequate privacy in the deep forest. "Tarp Talk" always began with a mentor or parent story. Then teens volunteered to recall and share positive vignettes from their childhood—all lightly focused on the day's curriculum agenda. We designed the formal curriculum into lightly sketched and high participation drama episodes which portrayed teen dilemmas and cast problem life situations in the highest humor we could create.

## Rites of Separation

Teens actually left their Old Status behind when they signed on for the weeklong rugged backpacking trip in the Red River Gorge of Eastern Kentucky. Watch the week unfold by tracing its marker events across the Zahniser diagram you first met in chapter 2. Turn back to the diagram if you want to follow it as you read the description of our weeklong rite of passage structure.

On arrival, during registration, our campers' Rite of Separation was marked by the gift of freshly hewn walking sticks. Then trail family leaders guided the campers each day to revisit some painful childhood experience and to carve a secret symbol of that experience into the appropriate "year band" they had first carved into the stick. These "revisit the pain" assignments were given at the 10:30 break each morning. Then, during the day's rest stops, the teens found relaxing times to remember specific instances of humiliation, pain, and regret that they would like to leave behind as they embraced the adult destiny ahead of them. We deliberately planned this "silent revisitation" with no conversation ever scheduled to magnify the pain or humiliation. Carving secret symbols in the year bands turned out to be a natural and relaxing occupation for the rest stops.

We chose the Liminal Task of remembering childhood sorrows to bring "bloodless pain" to each kid. Virtually all tribal cultures observe rites of passage which involve spilling blood and requiring silent surrender to contrived ritual pain.

We chose the silent carving task instead of an oral storytelling strategy because we did not want to add power to the story by inviting its public or even trail family disclosure. The young campers did not know, but we had plans to burn the sticks ceremonially—to sacrifice their childhood pain and sorrow—as a pre-condition for presenting their adult status to them in the night of ritual dedication.[1]

## Liminal Phase

Our major contribution during the Liminal Phase was to orchestrate both parent stories about the teens and positive observations of newly-acquainted trail leader mentors and ministers. The "heavy" curriculum consisted of both parents' and mentors' candor about what our graduate ministry students remembered as adult secrets for which they were unable to get straight answers by the end of high school. So, for example, the curriculum exposed the real truth about the relationship between responsibility and self-respect. And our students unraveled the human development mystery of sexual differentiation by which the kid's lifelong identity was created during the journey from conception to birth. Two days were devoted to parent stories which touched

---

[1]This "silent" approach to dealing with painful memories so as to ventilate without over-emphasizing it through over-exposing the details through oral telling, has corresponding implications in counseling and penal rehabilitation strategies. In counseling, the "subjective" memories take on "objective" and external form as they are reduced to written narrative or to symbol as in our carvings assigned for the walking sticks. Daniel N. Fader's *Hooked on Books* (New York: Putnam, 1968) describes a strategy used in Michigan with status offenders, young felons, in which they were required to fill four pages per day with written material, even if they had to copy the words from magazines or books. They eventually worked through their anger and their paralysis and wrote important personal "story" and poetry and song as well.

off celebration about each teen's conception and unique identity as a man or as a woman. The student mentors described the mystery of how to establish a lifetime-exclusive love relationship. Parents were invited to report on the power of the pair bonding process that led to intimacies of marriage and the birth of children. Student mentors told of their own deep awakenings of feelings of love and of the pair-bonding path to their engagements or marriages.

One trail family actually presented a summary rap of the week's secrets in a final evening celebration of remembering and sharing—all accurately translated and enveloped with humor. The whole weeklong event was reduced to a remarkable video record which we have called, *A Summer's Passage: Toward Freedom and Responsibility.*

## Rites of Reincorporation

We designed Thursday night for the surprise rite of passage ritual process. In tribal cultures the rite often has elements of surprise such as kidnapping and abduction. But we have absolutely no tolerance for pranks at anybody's expense, so we took the teens down to the wire without their knowing how their journey into adulthood would occur. These now well-seasoned campers were bonded to each other and to their mentors by hours of story sharing and vulnerable questioning and teaching. They were full of new information shared confidentially and discreetly. On Thursday evening the usual time of drama and singing gave way to instructions to wait by trail families until our designated mentor called for each family to approach the fire.

The Rite was designed to move with high drama. In groups of four and five, all sixteen teens entered the forest clearing not far from Sky Bridge. Each was blindfolded, and each was escorted by a parent or by a weeklong adult mentor. A small campfire crackled.

For five days, knowledgeable adults had tutored these kids in life's secrets. Together they had hiked between six and ten miles each day. They had cooked together. And they had told their own best life stories, talking into the night revealing their best life memories. They had carved symbols of worst memories and shame episodes within the year-bands laid out along the full length of now-handsome walking sticks. Each teen grasped the arm of the parent or mentor and used the ornately carved walking stick much as a blind person would do, checking the path and the obstacles with the now familiar and beautiful sticks. For each, the liturgy was the same.

The scenario played out with the liturgist Steve Brooks and the mentor team of two—Lisa Dout-Thompson and Mark Hale—orchestrating the steps of initiation within the circle of light produced by the campfire. The three leaders, Steve, Lisa, and Mark had designed the week's curriculum and actually wrote the ritual.

As each candidate's name was called, a parent or a student-mentor answered first questions for each candidate. These adult presenters provided the teen's name and told a brief story from their own experience with the kid; a story which they offered as proof that the teen was now ready to advance to adult freedom and responsibility. Here are highlights from the empowering liturgy.

The liturgist announced:

> This trail camp is more than a week's journey or pilgrimage.
> You can make it your giant step, your week of passage into significant adult status, power, and responsibility.
> In past generations, in every culture, our ancestors celebrated a ritual of passage.
> Children were taught the secrets of the adult world and the duties of the man or of the woman.
> But we were uprooted long ago from that tradition:
> Our culture declined.
> Our traditions have been neglected.
> Now, our families have been shaken;
> Some have even been broken.

Then all parents and mentors intoned:

> Yes, my child, this week can be for you a "Mid-summer's night of passage."
> Let this be for you a week of fire, of mystery, and of precious sacrament.
> Let this be your first moment "to see life steadily and see it whole,"
> —responsibility as pleasure more than duty,
> —life as gift, celebration, and sacrament to God,
> —your manhood/womanhood as sacred, as holy to God,
> —your dream of love and family as a God-given vision.
> We release you. We empower you to grasp your future.
> Will you give all that you are to Jesus?

Now the teens were prompted to take the challenge and to affirm that surrender. "I will, God helping me. I will do it."

Each candidate then heard words from the liturgist who stood face-to-face with a handful of campers. Looking first at one, then at another, Steve forcefully interrogated them about their understanding of their identity and origin:

> Who do you think you are?
> Where did you come from?
> Did you create yourself out of nothing?
> Why do you think you were created and placed on this planet?
> What do you plan to do with your life and energy?
> Have you considered that you alone are responsible for choosing what to do with your life?
> Are you ready to take hold of your full responsibility as an adult, or do you want to remain forever a child?

Now Steve, Lisa, and Mark spoke in chorus:

> Come with us.
> We are reaching down inside of you.
> We are reaching deep to restore your lost human inheritance.
> We are putting you in touch with secrets.
> These are secrets of The Holy.
> You will take hold of adult freedom and responsibility.

Once again the liturgist shook down candidates' intentions:

> Are you ready to leave your childhood ways behind and to move into manhood/womanhood?
> Are you willing to take on the privileges and rights of the adult world as well as its duties and responsibilities? Answer me: Are you?

As Steve's eyes and each camper's eyes met, every teen responded: "I am."

The liturgist continued:

> Then you must give up your childhood.
> You must release its feelings of weakness, of embarrassment, and shame.
> You may now celebrate your parents' and mentors' empowering, the secrets they have shared with you.
> Will you surrender the pain and sorrow of your childhood?
> Will you give it all to Jesus?
> If so, then place your walking stick with all of its history of pain and sorrow on the fire.

We held our breaths. Would these young women and men sacrifice their crafted symbols of pain and sorrow into the fire? The beauty of those "pain and sorrow" carvings were a treasure. Would they do it? But they did. For two hours they came, and each of them placed carved walking sticks on the fire:

| | |
|---|---|
| Michael Anderson | Linda Rosales |
| David Brooks | Faith Shorthouse |
| Brandon Dawalt | Chris Stone |
| David Giles | Craig Stone |
| Daniel Gill | Jacob Tschetter |
| John Mark Kennedy | Susanne Valk |
| Dale Kenney | Joseph Wilson |
| Rhonda Keys | Kyle Winner |

Then it was time for the promise of surrender to be acted out in full view of the growing crowd of initiated candidates, mentors, and parents. The liturgist confronted each camper:

> Just as Jesus died on the cross so we could put our sins behind us,
> Take your place on this cross where we have more to say to you.
> Your "crucifixion" will help you to remember
>     this night when you put away your childhood.

At this point each candidate was led to a handcrafted cross tied to a tree. Its platform was about eighteen inches off the ground. Standing on that platform, with arms tied to the crossbeam with red towels, the "cruci-form" emphasized the candidate's vulnerability to the entire community—arms tied slightly higher than their shoulders.

Now it was the liturgist, the mentor team, along with all remaining mentors and parents who intoned the ritual in chorus, inserting the candidate's name throughout the ceremony of empowerment:

> We dedicate you, [Name]
>     — to God the Father, who created you in the image of God
>        male/female.
>     — to Jesus, who died to forgive your sins and who is God's image
>        to all of us—He is both Bride and Groom.
>     — to the Holy Spirit, whose breath can make you fully holy and
>        fully human.
>     — alive to your fingertips as God's blessed man/woman!
> Will you always "trust in the Lord with all your heart and not lean on
>     your own childish understanding?"

Then the liturgist repeated, with full eye contact, demanding an answer,

"Will you trust in God?" and the teen-now-adult responded, some through tears:

"I will."

The liturgist persisted: "Will you always 'acknowledge God,' asking Jesus to 'make your paths straight'? [See Proverbs 3:5-6.] Answer me, will you?"

Teen: "I will, God helping me, I will!"

With these answers, the mentor team now assisted each novitiate to stand down to the ground, offering one of the towels to manage tears if they were visible. Then each was escorted to a plastic ground cloth, helped to lie down alongside other trail family teens. Each candidate's face was covered with a towel, symbolizing the death of childhood and the coming resurrection of the new adult. With each candidate's face covered, the liturgist now gave a final commissioning:

> 2 Timothy 2:11-13 says,
> "If we died with Jesus, we will also live with him.
> If we endure, we will also reign with him.
> If we disown him, he will also disown us;
> If we are faithless, he will remain faithful, because he cannot break his
>     own promise."
> You alone will choose the paths you take in life.
> You are free to choose the tough and narrow road to glory, fulfillment
>     of your dream, and eternal life.
> Or you may choose the easy road and go with the flow toward shame,
>     guilt, and destruction.
> When you were a child,
> you talked like a child.
> You thought like a child.
> You made decisions like a child.
> Now that you are fully empowered as an adult,
> you have put away your childish ways of
>     talking, thinking, and making decisions!

Then, helping them to their feet, Steve, Lisa, and Mark were the first to greet them with affirmations and to present them on their feet to the community. Steve empowered them in the presence of all of us:

> 1 Timothy 4:12 says,
> "Don't let anyone look down on you
>     because you are young,
> But set an example for everyone by your speech,
> by your life,

by your love,
by your faith and your purity of life."

And in Saint Paul's Second Letter to young Timothy,
    chapter 2, verse 22, he goes on:
"Flee youthful passions like the plague,
but pursue what is godly:
righteousness, faith, love, and peace,
along with all of those good people
    who call on the name of Jesus out of a pure heart."

Then Steve called for the entire crowd to raise shouts of celebration, to greet the new initiates to adult freedom and responsibility. After appropriate community singing to seal the moment, the liturgist made a final presentation:

It is my privilege to present each of you with a
new walking stick, fresh, with a lifetime of adventure and
victory to be carved into it. Go now with God's grace on you!

Mark Hale had handcrafted the new walking sticks in the shop of Brookside School where he was a part-time employee. They were made of cherry-stained rod stock, featured a leather grip, and carried a hand painted "logo," which read, "DEADicated, August 12, 1991."

The ceremony of the summer's passage began at seven o'clock. We continued for more than two hours. Each kid's empowering story told by a parent or mentor was unique. The parade of walking sticks bearing their childhood carvings of pain and shame were glorious in uniqueness, but alike in another way: they were full of carvings—secret symbols of pain and sorrow from early years to the present moment.

Our summer's passage teens came from widely different households. Three were from institutional foster care. Some were from blended families and came with a step-parent or accepted a ministry student counselor as mentor. Most were from mother-father-kid households. One had insisted that his father not accompany him, wanting to do this trip on his own. The teens were alike in their eagerness and hope for an adult life worth living. They were alike in their vitality and spontaneity. And they were identical in their willingness to lay aside their childhoods with their regrets and pain and to embrace the domain of their emerging adulthood. All of them embraced that covenant. We listened. We watched. We celebrated with them.

We crafted an initiation ritual from Christian tradition complete with pain, humiliation, and blood. But the episode from Christian history included a major transition—a liminal state—followed by a "death, burial, and live again" series of peak experiences offering continuing celebration. We built the experience around the suffering, death, burial, and resurrection of Jesus.

## Other Models for Initiation

Matthias Zahniser has suggested in "Ritual Process and Christian Discipling" that a rite of passage might easily be constructed around the episode of Jesus' great temptation in the wilderness, in his struggle with evil.[2]

In May of 1995, Steve Venable earned his Doctor of Ministry degree at Asbury Seminary, and filed in evidence his research dissertation which reported a study of *Mountain Cathedrals: An Exploratory Study of Spiritual Growth in Teen-Agers Through Backpacking*.[3] He designed the experimental curriculum around issues leading up to Jesus' crucifixion. Each day the campers reflected on those issues in private "solo times." They followed careful instructions in structured writing tasks—closely reminiscent of the solitary reflection during Jesus' wilderness temptation. Together, Steve and I have reported our collective wisdom in *How to Use Camping Experiences in Religious Education: Transformation Through Christian Camping*.[4] Steve also gives a full liturgy for a rite of passage used with his backpackers in the Rocky Mountains in that book.

Rob Neel once designed a class project with me in "Discipleship Development in the Home." He called his curriculum *Sons of Thunder*. It featured plans for a weekend retreat in which men would initiate teenage boys into manhood. Neel's biblical model was that of Jesus naming and calling out the disciples. In *Sons of Thunder* fathers participated, but not in the surprise "calling out" from the boys' homes Friday afternoon just as school had ended. The boys' mothers were recruited to play the "resister" role, insisting that their sons were "only boys," not suited for the men's retreat; the van was

---

[2]See A.H. Mathias Zahniser, "Ritual Process and Christian Discipline." *Missiology: An International Review*, Vol. XIX, No. 1, January 1991, Wilmore, KY 40390. In the article Zahniser proposes using the Great Temptation as a model for a rite of passage.

[3]See Stephen Fletcher Venable, *Mountain Cathedrals: An Exploratory Study of Spiritual Growth in Teen-Agers Through Backpacking*. Wilmore: Asbury Theological Seminary, 1995 Doctor of Ministry Dissertation.

[4]Stephen F. Venable and Donald M. Joy, *How to Use Camping Experiences in Religious Education: Transformation Through Christian Camping*. Birmingham, Religious Education Press, 1998.

waiting outside to take the boys away. This *Sons of Thunder* weekend retreat was designed for initiating young men into the adult men's fellowship complete with opportunities for making a response to the claims of Jesus on their emerging adult lives.

Hule Goddard, looking at the family and its developmental needs, has designed rites of passage at the close of each age level as a marker point of entry into the next. In a career in which he had oversight for families in a full-service congregation, Hule orchestrated parent-kid rituals by coaching some of the early rites as home events. He observes that by middle school, the transition points deserve community empowering.

Lynn Shmidt came out of Africa, tracking down the human development emphasis in his studies with me. He enrolled in my courses in a specific search for a way to sanctify a powerful ritual passage from the dominant culture in his South Africa environment. As he studied ritual passage across cultures, he saw the importance of the ritual bridge from childhood to adulthood. In the political environment of his medical missionary assignment, Islamic tradition (the dominant culture) required that boys pass through a week of retreat at the onset of puberty, during which time they would be circumcised, the mark of their initiation into adult male responsibility and opportunity. The weeklong retreat allowed recovery time from the painful surgery, often done under septic conditions. So as an ardent evangelist and a medical professional, Lynn saw unusual opportunity to capitalize on an existing dominant ritual event for boys. He contemplated that by looking at the Abrahamic establishment of circumcision as a mark of God's people, he could design a profoundly Judeo-Christian retreat. The Christian ritual would parallel, but surpass, the dominant Islamic culture's ritual by grounding it in the Abraham, Isaac, and Ishmael tradition and by completing the hygienic surgical procedure under antiseptic conditions required by Christian ministry standards.

In *A Summer's Passage: Toward Freedom and Responsibility*[5] we reversed the historical sequence and followed the teens' "resurrection" with a community celebration of Holy Communion. It is clear that an alternative ritual process

---

[5]*A Summer's Passage: Toward Freedom and Responsibility*, a video-report of the 1991 rite-of-passage adventure with teens is available on loan, but not for reproduction or sale, and must be regarded as a documentary of an experience made available only for research and study purposes. Contact the Center for the Study of the Family at 600 North Lexington Avenue, Wilmore, KY 40390, for schedule and costs of lending.

could be designed by planning for the "Last Supper" scenario to invite a final sharing of secrets and appealing for faithfulness before moving to crucifixion, death, and resurrection. Or, the "Last Supper" might be a sufficient initiation event if fully developed, with the sharing of the bread dipped in broth as the fidelity test to pass.

Washing feet in the "Last Supper" episode might be isolated out and made into the ritual event by itself. As a culminating event to a retreat or work camp in which personal histories have been shared, we have found a liturgy of servanthood through washing one another's feet to have powerful bonding and affirming effects.

Every tradition has additional heroes around whose transforming experiences a rite of passage might be designed. But here are some of the key observations I have made across recent years as I look for effective ways to empower our young through community rites.

## Mentors Hold Special Leverage

When communities initiate to empower their young, two classes of adults emerge: parents and significant elders beyond the family. In typical third world, traditional, or stone-age cultures the family prepares and presents the candidate for initiation, whether female or male. But it is a priest or a mentor or a midwife who welcomes the daughter or son into the world of adults.

In this book I have made a strong case for families to encourage them to stand against the popular culture in empowering their kids. But there is both ancient tradition and current data to underscore the effectiveness and special leverage which comes into play when community leaders, ministers, and other mentors become the empowering authorities for your kids.

Steve Venable tested his teen initiates in a "Path to Adulthood" rites of passage experience in his *Mountain Cathedrals* Rocky Mountain backpacking adventure using a standard spiritual wellness test. They took a pre-trip reading on camper scores before the weeklong trip. Then campers were retested at four- and twelve-week intervals following the rite of passage trip. Approximately half of the teens had been trail camping with a parent. The remaining teens found mentors in counselor staff unrelated to them. While the first scores were virtually identical, the teens with non-family mentors tested out with higher spiritual wellness scores at both four and twelve weeks after the experience.

Robert Bly has observed that the job of a parent and the job of a mentor or a minister are very different tasks.[6] Parents are responsible for seeing that you survive to grow up, that nothing bad happens to you, that you do not starve, and that you learn how to be civilized. Ministers and mentors, on the other hand, are chosen by the young protégé. They are chosen for inspirational reasons, especially as models and teachers who are expected to polish specific skills at the invitation of the novice. The minister's or mentor's job is to bless, to refine the skills, and to encourage. When a minister or mentor slips into parenting behaviors, the effectiveness of the minister or mentor in shaping the novice tends to be seriously impaired.

Let me put the diagram from chapter 1 into an updated form to remind all of us that just as the magic of childhood imprints the child with the parent's care, consistency, and affection, so also mentors are like midwives to teens and young adults. Walk through the desire cycle and think of ways you have been shaped by a mentor. And ask whether you are willing to be a parent to your own children—focusing on their primary care—and willing to be a mentor to other people's teens and emerging adults.

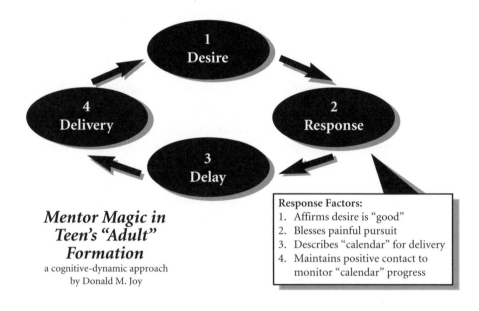

**Mentor Magic in Teen's "Adult" Formation**
a cognitive-dynamic approach
by Donald M. Joy

**Response Factors:**
1. Affirms desire is "good"
2. Blesses painful pursuit
3. Describes "calendar" for delivery
4. Maintains positive contact to monitor "calendar" progress

---

[6]See Robert Bly, *A Gathering of Men*, with host Bill Moyers on PBS as they explore the crisis in men's formation in the USA. Bly distinguishes in that conversation between the task of the father and the task of the mentor, who he calls the "male mother" which every young man needs.

## Expeditions Predict Best

While a Shin Byu boy may be transformed into a Burmese Buddhist priest in three days,[7] and a South Africa Nuer boy may receive the Gar initiation rite consisting of a series of halo incisions denoting his new status as a man in a matter of minutes, both are marked with intentional rituals of shaving and cutting, leaving visible physical marks which last for months or a lifetime.

Community rituals today which leave permanent change tend to include these elements:

a. separation from familiar surroundings, friends, and family;

b. entering into an uncertain, ambiguous experience, normally with significant ambivalence;

c. extensive community-building;

d. trust-based revelations of personal history and confidential dreams and hopes;

e. hammered out in long days of hard work completed through necessary cooperation;

f. all sealed by an intentional ritual in a climactic ceremony; and

g. followed by a ritual ending of the initiation and the intensive community and the working relationships.

It has been our experience that significant change in the moral-emotional-spiritual readiness of teens does not occur before the fourth day of a work mission or a trail camp. Evidently that is the minimum time required before the community base is established. That base is necessary as the foundation for targeted moral-emotional-spiritual transformation denoted by any rite of reincorporation into the adult community.

I find that time is a non-negotiable real factor in establishing trust in any group. With lunch groups of students committed to spiritual formation and mutual support, the rule of thumb has turned out across more than twenty years to be this: Candor and easy trust requires a minimum of hours invested equal to the number of participants in the group, and with absolute perfect commitment to attendance. Unaccountable absences build suspicion of lack of commitment, lack of priority. Hence unexplained absences suggest low-

---

[7]Professor Mathias Zahniser cites the Shin Byu Buddhist ritual through which a young pre-pubescent enters the monastery in elaborate ceremony. See footnote 2 on page 107.

priority and carelessness with the group, so raise a question about confidentiality and safety when the intermittently absent member returns.[8]

## Intentional Curriculum Pays Off

So whether in a missional work crew or a backcountry camping trip, we consistently build voluntary story sharing into the early days. We never subject a member to confrontation in order to get participation or to pry for more detail than is volunteered. When counselors as ministers and mentors lead in the story sharing, the novices tend to move easily into high trust revelations and candor as protégés.

Listen to this disclosure from a recently confirmed young man from the Newman Center: "I know that Will and Randy will be surprised to hear this," Kirk shared at age 13, "because they know me at school. But I've known now for about a year that I am going to have to decide whether to accept God's call to become a priest. I've watched Jack and John here this week, and I guess if they can be ministers, I guess God could make me into a priest."

## Transformation Continues

A teen discipleship week, a confirmation retreat, or any other ritual passage event deserves to be planned to include time and agendas for building a high trust community. Get action tasks, story sharing, and full cooperation tasks into the curriculum of experience early and often. The rites of separation and of reincorporation can often be carefully designed as peak experiences at both ends of the "working sweat" of the liminal phase.

## Discomfort Is a Key

I'm afraid my advance equipment notices to campers has failed to convey the rugged nature of a week or more on the Sheltowee Trace of Daniel Boone National Forest. When a crew of a dozen youth and their youth pastors Max and Liz Mertz arrived from Abilene, Texas, we met a vanload of affluent and gorgeous kids. Expensive sports outfits were everywhere. And by morning, the

---

[8]See my *Men Under Construction*, in which I report on issues men have named in my 27 years of hosting spiritual formation groups in my office over brown-bag lunch hours. There I also report (pages 71-73) on research I have conducted with these men which reveals the importance of confidential male friendships during the middle school years in predicting confident attachment and marriage before age 25. *Men Under Construction* is available from Evangel Publishing House, Nappanee, IN at 800-253-9315.

gossip was out: one of the young women from Abilene had brought a propane-fired hair curler to maintain her signature coiffure on the trail.

But on the third day she presented her sacred propane curler and other high-tech accessories to me. "Can you let me leave these on the chuck wagon for the rest of the trip?" she was asking. "I brought some things I don't want to carry any more."

By the end of the week, the relationships had been subjected to the leveling impact of trail camping and hard daily work. When the week closed with an elaborate service of Holy Communion, the bonding tears of spiritual reincorporation were everywhere.

One of those Abilene young men summarized it: "I knew I was pretty good at camping and all that stuff when I got here last week. But after our trail family was lost for one whole night and we went without two meals before you guys located us, I discovered that I am really a survivor! With a trail family like this, I could go through anything."

Jeff, one of the brightest young athletes ever to walk the trail with us, ignored our advice about the care of feet. After all, he was a cool jock and used his feet handily in high competition. By the end of the second day, he was in severe pain. His student leader sent him to me: "Mr. Joy, I think I need to have you look at my feet."

I had never seen such deep crevices in the broken flesh under the site of long-since broken blisters. He obviously had avoided the fresh water where I thought all of us had played under a waterfall and had been freshly bathed for the evening.

Jeff's feet were caked with sweat and dirt. So, taking my camp scissors from my wallet, I began to clear away the dying flesh. Jeff ground his teeth and endured my cleansing routine, then easily took a final painting with Mercurochrome. By morning he was able to walk without pain. But six months later at a winter retreat for Jeff's church, I watched him work quietly and effectively in recruiting three high school senior friends into first-time commitments to faith in Jesus. Jeff, the "Nike kid in the woods," had been transformed by a week of painful experience in our discipleship development through trail camping.

In this chapter I have wanted to offer the "community" empowering ritual models which add powerful leverage to family goals for launching your kids into freedom and responsibility. And as you reflect on the structure of this handbook, you will do well to accept the invitation to bless and empower kids, to go into early and direct competition with "the world, the flesh, and devil" to take back our children, and to initiate them into God's "very good" human creation of having dominion and taking responsibility for all of life.

## Connect with Community

As parents, ministers, and other mentors, you may want to assess the health and ability of the various agency systems to which you may turn to enter into a good conspiracy to empower and initiate our children. Churches have the greatest potential for such empowerment if they possess the authority for a family and its children. Other agencies such as the "Y," recreational leagues, the public school, private school, or home-school cluster often have great potential, but none has a year-long, lifelong network to sustain your child across the entire life span. If your extended family can be recruited to join in a family ritual of empowerment, you may be able to incorporate the empowerment ceremonies in conjunction with a reunion or a holiday which consistently brings this important system to full visibility.

Here are urgent priority qualities to insist on in your most empowering system. I train youth, children's, adult, and pastoral ministry professionals, so my listing is easily applicable to what you deserve to find or to create in what some of us call a "full service" congregation:

**Systemic community**—Career ministry staff, volunteers, and recruited teachers and leaders of specialty groups all see the total congregation as the body of Christ in this place. This "systemic" view always sees the whole, not simply age-level or other specialty parts. Systematic organizations often specialize into airtight, sealed-off groupings.

The "whole Body" community will see great cohesion of diverse groups: age span, marital status, relative time spent in the community. This will mean that there are frequent exposure opportunities in which all come together, and where all celebrate the specialty programs and goals of the many groups. The full-service congregation looks for ways for specialty groups to serve each other. Only when systemic community is very strong can any organization undertake initiation of its members through the life cycle.

**Unconditional respect**—No congregation or other community is worth trusting unless every person is seen as irreplaceable, unique, and of highest value. Look for both words and actions which show respect for the entire life span of membership. How seriously does the community address specialty needs of early childhood and of senior citizen members? What program opportunities are focused on those specialty needs?

Respect in philosophy and program tend to be matched by equal respect—or disrespect—for specialty age groups in their ways of speaking and acting toward each other. In high respect communities, you will hear people speak to each other across specialty boundaries affectionately and by name. In low respect, you will hear critical and derisive comments about other specialty programs or groups, and will not be surprised when people turn on other members of their own specialty group, subjecting them to harassment, ridicule, and pranks. Any prank which leaves the victim to clean up the mess or recover from the humiliation alone is a sign of low commitment to the value of people in that community.

**Mature leaders**—Whether they are career professionals or elected and appointed for leadership within the community, these people need to show signs in speech and behavior that they are settled and clear in their identity and calling.

Youth ministry attracts many professionals who have deep respect for adults who blessed them and empowered them during the difficult years of middle school and high school. Those are years when most of us recall that we must have been granted a lot of respect to offset our clumsiness and naiveté. The executive youth minister, as well as the youth leader volunteer team, all need to be people who have resolved the teen-years dilemmas about vocation, career, intimacy, and identity in spiritual grounding.

If a youth leader has not escaped the cultural and electronic media "lifelong adolescent party" syndrome, you will not want your children to grow up in search of identity around such a person. Examine any youth program to see whether it is programmed for extravagant and costly entertainment—a sort of holy "party community"—and whether the view is that "everybody owes us this party." Such immature adolescent programming environments show verbal and behavioral disrespect for all other age or specialty groups, and tend to emphasize "value based on their own egocentric age group." They will demand space, time, and money to fund their pleasure, but will rarely get on board with an intergenerational mission or service project. This low-respect, high adolescent leader and age specialty group will insist in every way that their people and their program are the heart and center of the life of the community.

You can see that a congregation or other agency that is ready to respond to your appeal for "rites of passage," "initiation" and "empowerment" of your teens will need to be ready by virtue of the quality of life they maintain for the entire intergenerational family. Start now to create such an empowering full-service community where you have membership and influence.

In such a community there are professionals equipped with both training and experience in respecting the life span of human growth and development. Such leaders see the unusual opportunities for discipleship recruitment and development over the years. You can expect to develop a youth ministry environment which is devoted to service, work, and high adventure opportunities. Together, these experiences both initiate teens into full adult roles and responsibilities and bring them into significant transforming contact with life-empowering mentors and models beyond your own family.

# INDEX